NECTAR

21 DESIGNS

by Kim Hargreaves

DESIGNS
KIM HARGREAVES

PHOTOGRAPHY
GRAHAM WATTS

STYLING
KIM HARGREAVES

HAIR & MAKE-UP
DIANA FISHER

MODELS
FIONA BECK, NICHOLA RADCLIFFE & HANNAH WRIGHT

EDITOR
KATHLEEN HARGREAVES

EDITORIAL DESIGN
GRAHAM WATTS

LAYOUTS
ANGELA LIN

PATTERNS
KATHLEEN HARGREAVES, SUE WHITING & STELLA SMITH

LOCATION
FORM ARCHITECTURAL DESIGN & DEVELOPMENT
www.formgroup.co.uk

First published in 2008 by Kim Hargreaves, Intake Cottage, 26 Underbank Old Road, Holmfirth, West Yorkshire, HD9 1EA, England

British Library Cataloguing in Publication Data
A catalogue record for this book is available from the British Library

ISBN-10: 1-906487-01-0
ISBN-13: 978-1-906487-01-0

CONTENTS

THE DESIGNS

THE LOOK IS GRACEFUL AND FEMININE. THE PALETTE OF PEARL WHITES, BLOSSOM PINKS AND SILVER GREYS IS PALE BUT INTERESTING, WHILE HIGHLIGHTS OF LUSCIOUS BLOOMS AND OCEAN BLUE COMPLETE THIS DELICIOUS SUMMER BLEND.

MISTY — (ABOVE) AN A-LINE CARDIGAN WITH CABLES & EYELET DETAIL

NECTAR — (OPPOSITE) CHIC TUNIC WITH AN ELEGANT DRAPE

LAGOON — (ABOVE) AN UNDERSTATED TUNIC WITH BOAT NECK

DAWN — (OPPOSITE) OPENWORK CARDIGAN WITH GARTER STITCH TRIMS

DAWN — OPENWORK CARDIGAN WITH GARTER STITCH TRIMS

HONEY — FITTED TEXTURED CABLE JACKET WITH FULL SLEEVES

GLINT — (ABOVE) CROPPED SHRUG WITH SHORT SLEEVES

GLIMMER — (OPPOSITE) JACKET WITH DOUBLE BUTTONS & SLIGHTLY FLARED SLEEVES

RIPPLE — CLASSIC BUTTON THROUGH SWEATER

BREEZE — (ABOVE) LONG-LINE COAT WORKED IN A BASKET WEAVE STITCH

HARMONY — (OPPOSITE) GARTER STITCH CARDIGAN WITH LACE PEPLUM

SUNLIT — CABLE TUNIC WITH DEEP GARTER STITCH YOKE

FAVOUR — A-LINE CARDIGAN WITH CABLE PANELS & FULL SLEEVES

GLEE — FITTED TEXTURED PEPLUM JACKET WITH GARTER STITCH EDGINGS

ORCHID — FITTED JACKET WITH SHAPED PEPLUM

ORCHID — FITTED JACKET WITH SHAPED PEPLUM

GLINT — (ABOVE) CROPPED SHRUG WITH SINGLE BUTTON

JOY — (OPPOSITE) CLASSIC CARDIGAN WITH EYELET TEXTURE

DAPPLE — TUNIC WITH CABLE PANELS & DEEP GARTER STITCH NECKLINE

DAPPLE — TUNIC WITH CABLE PANELS & DEEP GARTER STITCH NECKLINE

FLICKER — SLOUCHY HAT WITH BEADED BAND

BREEZE — BASKET WEAVE COAT WITH SIDE VENTS & GARTER STITCH TRIM

TENDER — (ABOVE) CARDIGAN WITH FLOUNCE EDGINGS

FLICKER — (OPPOSITE) BEADED OPENWORK SLOUCHY HAT

ENCHANT — (ABOVE) SOFT SHORT SLEEVED SHRUG WORKED CUFF TO CUFF

GLISTEN — (OPPOSITE) FITTED BEADED WAISTCOAT WITH DEEP V-NECKLINE

JASMINE — FITTED SWEATER WITH DEEP GARTER STITCH YOKE & BUTTON DETAIL

JASMINE — FITTED SWEATER WITH DEEP GARTER STITCH YOKE & BUTTON DETAIL

THE PATTERNS

NECTAR

CHIC TUNIC WITH AN ELEGANT DRAPE

Recommendation
Suitable for the more experienced knitter
Please see pages 7 & 8 for photographs.

	XS	S	M	L	XL	XXL	
To fit	**81**	**86**	**91**	**97**	**102**	**109**	**cm**
bust	32	34	36	38	40	43	in

Rowan Classic Bamboo Soft
Photographed in Eider

10	11	11	12	12	13	x50gm

Needles
1 pair 3 ¼mm (no 10) (US 3) needles
1 pair 3 ¾mm (no 9) (US 5) needles

Tension
Before steaming: 24 sts and 30 rows to 10 cm measured over stocking stitch using 3 ¾ mm (US 5) needles.

Tension note:
The Bamboo Soft yarn relaxes after steaming; this opens the knitting and changes the tension by approximately one stitch in the width, but does not affect the rows (23 sts and 30 rows). Allowances have been made within the pattern for this change (see size diagram for after relaxing measurements).

BACK & FRONT (both alike)
Cast on 110 (116: 122: 128: 134: 142) sts using 3 ¾ mm (US 5) needles and beg with a K row cont in st st shaping sides as folls:
Work 20 (20: 22: 22: 22: 22) rows, ending with a WS row.
Next row (RS)(inc): K2, M1, K to last 2 sts, M1, K2.
112 (118: 124: 130: 136: 144) sts.
Work 9 rows.
Inc 1 st as before at each end of next row and 3 foll 8th rows, then on 3 foll 6th rows, and then on 3 foll 4th rows.
132 (138: 144: 150: 156: 164) sts.
Work 1 row, ending with a WS row.
Shape underarm
Inc 1 st as before at each end of next row and 3 foll alt rows, and then on foll row, ending with a WS row.
142 (148: 154: 160: 166: 174) sts.
Cast on 2 sts at beg of next 2 rows.
146 (152: 158: 164: 170: 178) sts.
Place a marker at each end of last row.
Work straight until armhole measures 16.5 (17.5: 17.5: 18.5: 19.5: 20.5) cm from markers, ending with a WS row.
Divide for neck
Next row (RS): K42 (44: 46: 48: 50: 53) and turn, leaving rem sts on a holder.
Work each side of neck separately.
Dec 1 st at neck edge on the next 4 rows.
38 (40: 42: 44: 46: 49) sts.
Work 1 row.
Leave rem sts on a holder.
With RS facing rejoin yarn to rem sts, cast off centre 62 (64: 66: 68: 70: 72) sts, work to end.
Complete to match first side, reversing shaping.

Lower edging
With RS of back facing, cast on edge uppermost and using 3 ¼ mm (US 3) needles, pick up and 87 (95: 101: 109: 115: 129) sts along lower edge of back.
Purl 1 row.
Row 1 (RS): K1, (P1, K1) to end.
Row 2: P1, (K1, P1) to end.
Row 3: Work as row 2.
Row 4: Work as row 1.
These 4 rows form the double moss st patt and are rep throughout.
Cont in patt shaping, shaping sides as folls:
Work 4 rows.
Inc 1 st at each end of next row.
89 (97: 103: 111: 117: 131) sts.
Keeping patt correct, work 7 rows.
Inc 1 st at each end of next row and 2 foll 8th rows.
95 (103: 109: 117: 123: 137) sts.
Work 11 (11: 13: 13: 15: 15) rows.
Cast off.
Work front lower edging to match.

Making up
Pin the pieces out, and **avoiding the lower edging completely**, steam gently without allowing the iron to touch the yarn.
Join shoulder seams as folls:
Join right shoulder seam
With the point of the needles facing from shoulder to neck edge, slip the stitches for the right back and front shoulders onto spare needles.
With the **WS** together and front facing, hold the back and front together in the left hand, and cast off the sts (on the **RS**) as folls:
Rejoin yarn to the neck edge, using a 3 ¾ mm (US 5) needle and taking one stitch from each needle together at the same time cast off all the sts.
Neck edging
With RS of front facing and using 3 ¼ mm (US 3) needles, pick up and knit 5 sts down the left front neck, 62 (64: 66: 68: 70: 72) sts across front neck, 5 sts up right front neck, 1 st at shoulder seam, 5 sts down down right back neck, 62 (64: 66: 68: 70: 72) sts across back neck and 5 sts up left back neck.
145 (149: 153: 157: 161: 165) sts.

Beg with a K row, work 4 rows in **rev** st st, ending with a **RS** row.
Cast of knitwise (on **WS**).

Join left shoulder seam

With the point of the needles facing from neck edge to shoulder, slip the stitches for the left back and front shoulders onto spare needles.
Cast off as given for right shoulder.
Join ends of neck edging neatly together.

Armhole edgings (both alike)

With RS facing and using 3 ¼ mm (US 3) needles, pick up and knit 43 (45: 45: 47: 49: 51) sts from marker to shoulder seam, 1 st on shoulder seam and 43 (45: 45: 47: 49: 51) down to marker.
87 (91: 91: 95: 99: 103) sts.
Purl 1 row.
Row 1 (RS): K1, (P1, K1) to end.
Row 2: P1, (K1, P1) to end.
Row 3: Work as row 2.
Row 4: Work as row 1.
These 4 rows form the double moss st patt and are rep throughout.
Work straight until edging measures 6 (6: 6.5: 6.5: 7: 7) cm, ending with a WS row.
Cast off in patt.
Join side and underarm seams.

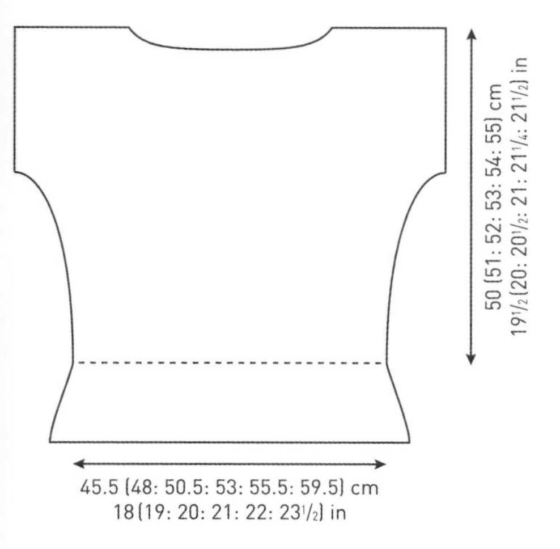

MISTY

A-LINE CABLED CARDIGAN WITH EYELET PANELS

Recommendation
Suitable for the knitter with a little experience
Please see page 9 for photograph.

	XS	S	M	L	XL	XXL	
To fit	**81**	**86**	**91**	**97**	**102**	**107**	**cm**
bust	32	34	36	38	40	42	in

Rowan Purelife Organic Cotton
Photographed in Logwood

8	9	9	10	10	11	x50gm

Needles
1 pair 3 ¼ mm (no 10) (US 3) needles
1 pair 3 ¾ mm (no 9) (US 5) needles
Cable needle

Buttons - 5

Tension
22 sts and 30 rows to 10 cm measured over stocking stitch using 3 ¾ mm (US 5) needles.

BACK
Cast on 131 (137: 141: 159: 165: 173) sts using 3 ¼ mm (US 3) needles and starting and ending where indicated work from chart for back setting sts as folls:
Chart row 1 (RS): P0 (1: 1: 1: 0: 0), (K1, P1) 7 (8: 9: 4: 6: 8) times, *P1, K6, P2, (K1, P1) 5 times; rep from * 4 (4: 4: 6: 6: 6) times more, P1, K6, P1, (P1, K1) 7 (8: 9: 4: 6: 8) times, P0 (1: 1: 1: 0: 0).
Chart row 2: P0 (1: 1: 1: 0: 0), (K1, P1) 7 (8: 9: 4: 6: 8) times, *K1, P6, (K1, P1) 6 times; rep from * 4 (4: 4: 6: 6: 6) times more, K1, P6, K1, (P1, K1) 7 (8: 9: 4: 6: 8) times, P0 (1: 1: 1: 0: 0).
These 2 rows set the sts.
Cont until chart row 6 completed, ending with a WS row.
Change to 3 ¾ mm (US 5) needles.
Cont from chart, working lace panels as folls:
Chart row 7 (RS): P15 (18: 20: 10: 13: 17), (K6, P13) 5 (5: 5: 7: 7: 7) times, K6, P15 (18: 20: 10: 13: 17).
Chart row 8: K8 (11: 13: 3: 6: 10), yon, K2tog tbl, K5, P6, (K6, yon, K2tog tbl, K5, P6) 5 (5: 5: 7: 7: 7) times, K6, yon, K2tog tbl, K7 (10: 12: 2: 5: 9).
These 2 rows set the stitches for the patt.
Cont until chart row 14 completed, ending with a WS row.
Cont working the 8 row patt rep until 9 reps in all completed, ending with a WS row.
Work 7 more rows in patt, ending with a **RS** row. **
Next row (WS)(dec): Patt 13 (16: 18: 8: 11: 15), K2tog, (P2tog tbl, P2, P2tog, K2tog tbl, patt 9, K2tog) 5 (5: 5: 7: 7: 7) times, P2tog tbl, P2, P2tog, K2tog tbl, patt to end.
107 (113: 117: 127: 133: 141) sts.
Cont working the 8 row lace pattern as before over the centre 9 sts of each panel and **at the same time** 'twist' the cables on the next row and every foll 8th row, i.e. every row 1 of the lace patt, as folls:
Patt row 1 (RS): P14 (17: 19: 9: 12: 16), (C4B, P11) 3 (3: 3: 4: 4: 4) times, (C4F, P11) 2 (2: 2: 3: 3: 3) times, C4F, P14 (17: 19: 9: 12: 16).
Patt row 2: K8 (11: 13: 3: 6: 10), yon, K2tog tbl, K4, P4, (K5, yon, K2tog tbl, K4, P4) 5 (5: 5: 7: 7: 7) times, K5, yon, K2tog tbl, K7 (10: 12: 2: 5: 9).
Patt row 3: P14 (17: 19: 9: 12: 16), (K4, P11) 5 (5: 5: 7: 7: 7) times, K4, P14 (17: 19: 9: 12: 16).
These 3 rows set the stitches for the lace cable patt.
Keeping lace patt correct and twisting cables on every 8th row, cont until 8 rows of lace cable patt completed, and then for **M, L, XL & XXL sizes only,** work 4 more rows, ending with a WS row.
Shape armholes
Keeping patt correct throughout cont as folls:
Cast off 4 (4: 4: 5: 5: 6) sts at beg of next 2 rows.
99 (105: 109: 117: 123: 129) sts.
Dec 1 st at each end of next 3 (3: 5: 5: 5: 5) rows and 3 (4: 2: 4: 5: 6) foll alt rows, and then on foll 4th row.
85 (89: 93: 97: 101: 105) sts.
Patt note: On the **XXL size** take the 2 cable sts at the armhole edge into rev st st.
Work straight until armhole measures 18 (19: 19: 20: 21: 22) cm, ending with a WS row.
Shape shoulders and back neck
Cast off 9 (9: 9: 9: 10: 10) sts at beg of next 2 rows.
Cast off 8 (9: 9: 9: 9: 10) sts, work until there are 12 (12: 13: 13: 13: 13) sts on right needle and turn, leaving rem sts on a holder.
Work each side of neck separately.
Cast off 4 sts at beg of next row.
Cast off rem 8 (8: 9: 9: 9: 9) sts.
With RS facing rejoin yarn to rem sts, cast off centre 27 (29: 31: 35: 37: 39) sts, work to end.
Complete to match first side, reversing shaping.

Left front

Cast on 74 (77: 79: 88: 91: 95) sts using 3 ¼ mm (US 3) needles and starting and ending where indicated work from chart for left front setting sts as folls:

Chart row 1 (RS): P0 (1: 1: 1: 0: 0), (K1, P1) 7 (8: 9: 4: 6: 8) times, *P1, K6, P2, (K1, P1) 5 times; rep from * 1 (1: 1: 2: 2: 2) times more, P1, K6, P1, (P1, K1) 7 times.

Chart row 2: (K1, P1) 7 times, *K1, P6, (K1, P1) 6 times; rep from * 1 (1: 1: 2: 2: 2) times more, K1, P6, K1, (P1, K1) 7 (8: 9: 4: 6: 8) times, P0 (1: 1: 1: 0: 0).

These 2 rows set the sts.

Cont until chart row 6 completed, ending with a WS row.

Change to 3 ¾ mm (US 5) needles.

Cont from chart, working lace panels as folls:

Chart row 7 (RS): P15 (18: 20: 10: 13: 17), (K6, P13) 2 (2: 2: 3: 3: 3) times, K6, P9, (K1, P1) 3 times.

Chart row 8: (P1, K1) 3 times, K2, yon, K2tog tbl, K5, P6, (K6, yon, K2tog tbl, K5, P6) 2 (2: 2: 3: 3: 3) times, K6, yon, K2tog tbl, K7 (10: 12: 2: 5: 9).

These 2 rows set the stitches for the patt and the front band.

Keeping six sts at front edge in double moss st, cont in patt rep the 8 row rep, until left front matches back to **, ending with a **RS** row.

Next row (WS)(dec): Patt 13, K2tog, (P2tog tbl, P2, P2tog, K2tog tbl, patt 9, K2tog) 2 (2: 2: 3: 3: 3) times, P2tog tbl, P2, P2tog, K2tog tbl, patt to end. 62 (65: 67: 72: 75 :79) sts.

Keeping the front edge stitches correct, cont working the 8 row lace pattern as before over the centre 9 sts of each panel and **at the same time** 'twist' the cables on the next row and every foll 8th row, i.e. every row 1 of the lace patt, as folls:

Patt row 1 (RS): P14 (17: 19: 9: 12: 16), (C4B, P11) 2 (2: 2: 3: 3: 3) times, C4B, P8, patt to end.

Patt row 2: Patt 6, K2, yon, K2tog tbl, K4, P4, (K5, yon, K2tog tbl, K4, P4) 2 (2: 2: 3: 3: 3) times, K5, yon, K2tog tbl, K7 (10: 12: 2: 5: 9).

Patt row 3: P14 (17: 19: 9: 12: 16), (K4, P11) 2 (2: 2: 3: 3: 3) times, K4, P8, patt to end.

These 3 rows set the stitches for the lace cable patt.

Cont until left front matches back to beg of armhole shaping, ending with a WS row.

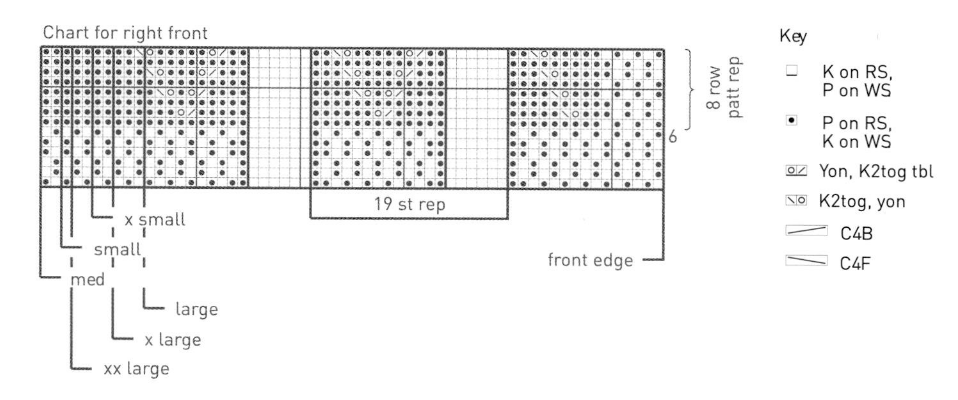

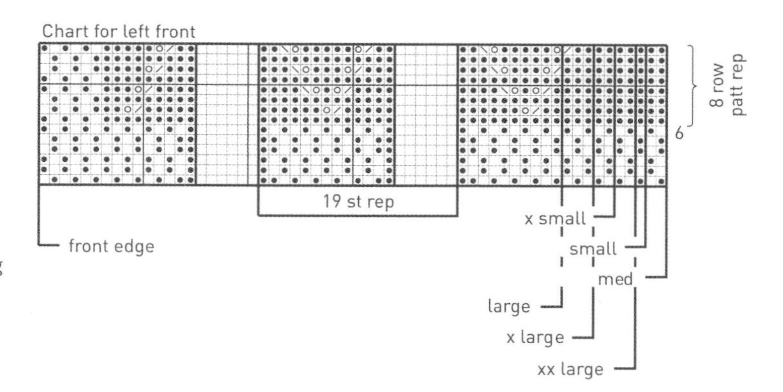

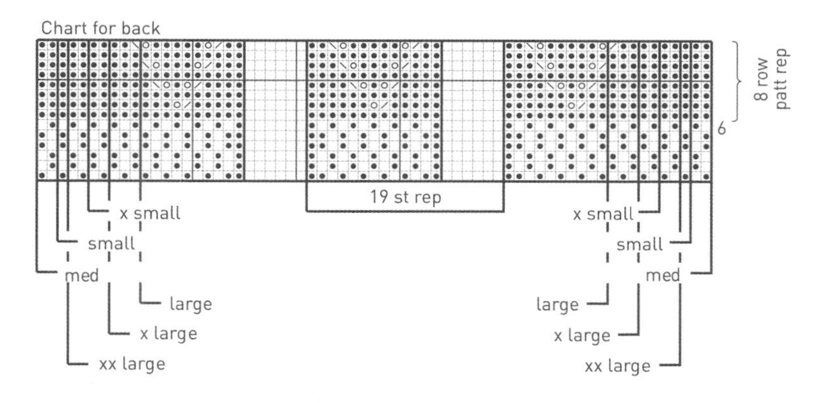

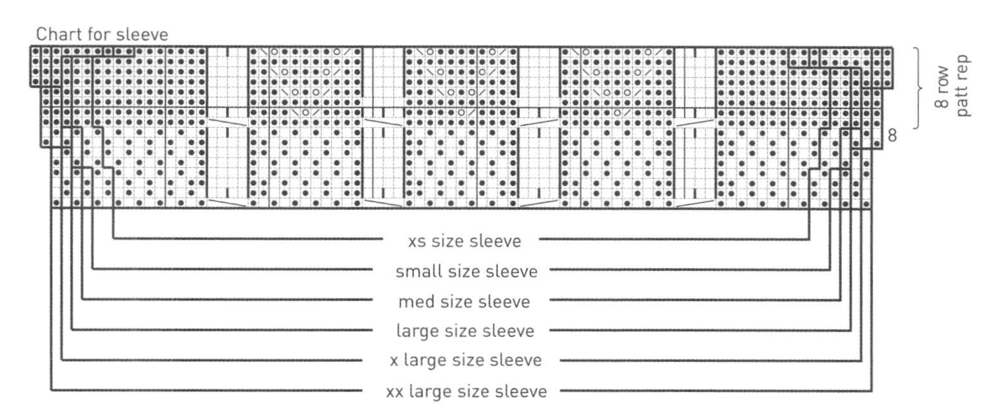

Shape armhole

Keeping patt correct throughout cont as folls:
Cast off 4 (4: 4: 5: 5: 6) sts at beg of next row.
58 (61: 63: 67: 70: 73) sts.
Work 1 row.
Dec 1 st at armhole edge of next 3 (3: 5: 5: 5: 5) rows and 3 (4: 2: 4: 5: 6) foll alt rows, and then on foll 4th row.
51 (53: 55: 57: 59: 61) sts.
Work straight until front is 22 (22: 24: 24: 26: 26) rows shorter than back to shoulder shaping, ending with a WS row.

Shape front neck

Next row (RS): Patt to last 14 (14: 14: 16: 16: 16) sts and turn leaving rem sts on a holder.
37 (39: 41: 41: 43: 45) sts.
Dec 2 sts at neck edge of next 2 (2: 2: 1: 1: 1) rows. 33 (35: 37: 39: 41: 43) sts.
Dec 1 st at neck edge of next 2 (4: 6: 7: 7: 9) rows, then on foll 5 (4: 3: 4: 5: 4) foll alt rows, and then on foll 4th row.
25 (26: 27: 27: 28: 29) sts.
Work straight until left front matches back to shoulder shaping, ending with a WS row.

Shape shoulder

Cast off 9 (9: 9: 9: 10: 10) sts at beg of next row and 8 (9: 9: 9: 9: 10) sts at beg of foll alt row.
Work 1 row.
Cast off rem 8 (8: 9: 9: 9: 9) sts.
Mark the position of 5 buttons, the first to come 6 rows below start of cable patt, the 5th will come 4 rows into neck band and rem 3 spaced evenly between.

Right front

Cast on 74 (77: 79: 88: 91: 95) sts using 3 ¼ mm (US 3) needles and starting and ending where indicated work from chart for right front setting sts as folls:
Chart row 1 (RS): (K1, P1) 7 times, *P1, K6, P2, (K1, P1) 5 times; rep from * 1 (1: 1: 2: 2: 2) times more, P1, K6, P1, (P1, K1) 7 (8: 9: 4: 6: 8) times, P0 (1: 1: 1: 0: 0).
Chart row 2: P0 (1: 1: 1: 0: 0), (K1, P1) 7 (8: 9: 4: 6: 8) times, *K1, P6, (K1, P1) 6 times; rep from * 1 (1: 1: 2: 2: 2) times more, K1, P6, K1, (P1, K1) 7 times.
These 2 rows set the sts.
Cont until chart row 6 completed, ending with a WS row.
Change to 3 ¾ mm (US 5) needles.
Cont from chart, working lace panels as folls:
Chart row 7 (RS): (P1, K1) 3 times, P9, (K6, P13) 2 (2: 2: 3: 3: 3) times, K6, P15 (18: 20: 10: 13: 17).
Chart row 8: K8 (11: 13: 3: 6: 10), yon, K2tog tbl, K5, P6, (K6, yon, K2tog tbl, K5, P6) 2 (2: 2: 3: 3: 3) times, K6, yon, K2tog tbl, K2, (K1, P1) 3 times.
These 2 rows set the stitches for the patt and the front band.
Complete as given for left front, twisting the cable in the opposite direction (as on back) and rev all shaping, and **at the same time** work 4 buttonholes to correspond with markers as folls:
Buttonhole row (RS): Patt 2 sts, patt 2tog, yon, patt to end.

Sleeves (both alike)

Cast on 67 (71: 73: 75: 77: 79) sts using 3 ¼ mm (US 3) needles and work lower edging as folls:
Row 1 (RS): P1 (1: 0: 1: 0: 1), (K1, P1) 4 (5: 6: 6: 7: 7) times, [C4B, P1, (K1, P1) 5 times] twice, C4F, P1, (K1, P1) 5 times, C4F, (P1, K1) 4 (5: 6: 6: 7: 7) times, P1 (1: 0: 1: 0: 1).
Row 2: K0 (0: 1: 0: 1: 0), (P1, K1) 4 (5: 5: 6: 6: 7) times, [K1, P4, K2, (P1, K1) 4 times] 3 times, K1, P4, K1, (K1, P1) 4 (5: 5: 6: 6: 7) times, K0 (0: 1: 0: 1: 0).
These 2 rows set the sts.
Cont from chart until chart row 8 completed, inc 1 st at each end of 5th (5th: 5th: 7th: 7th: 7th) row as indicated and ending with a WS row.
69 (73: 75: 77: 79: 81) sts.
Change to 3 ¾ mm (US 5) needles and keeping shaping correct cont until chart row 14 (14: 14: 16: 16: 16) completed ending with a WS row.
71 (75: 77: 79: 81: 83) sts.

Shape sleeve top

Keeping patt correct throughout shape sleeve top as folls:
Cast off 4 (4: 4: 5: 5: 6) sts at beg of next 2 rows.
63 (67: 69: 69: 71: 71) sts.
Dec 1 st at each end of next 3 rows and foll alt row.
55 (59: 61: 61: 63: 63) sts.
Work 3 rows.
Dec 1 st at each end of next and 4 (4: 4: 4: 4: 5) foll 4th rows, then on 4 (5: 5: 5: 6: 5) foll alt rows, and then on every foll row until 27 (29: 31: 31: 31: 31) sts rem.
Cast off.

Making up

Pin out the pieces, cover with a dry cloth and steam.
Leave knitting to set before removing pins.
Join shoulder seams using back stitch or mattress st if preferred.

Neck edging

With RS of right front facing and using 3 ¼ mm (US 3) needles, slip 14 (14: 14: 16: 16: 16) sts from holder onto right needle, rejoin yarn and pick up and knit 24 (25: 26: 26: 28: 28) sts up right front neck, 31 (33: 35: 39: 41: 43) sts across back and 24 (25: 26: 26: 28: 28) sts down left front, work in patt across 14 (14: 14: 16: 16: 16) sts on holder.
107 (111: 115: 123: 129: 131) sts.
Work in double moss st as folls:
Keeping double moss st patt correct, work 3 rows, ending with a WS row.
Next row (RS)(buttonhole): Work 2 sts, patt 2tog, yon, patt to end.
Work 2 rows, ending with a **RS** row.
Cast off in patt.
Join side and sleeve seams.
Set sleeves into armholes.
Sew on buttons to correspond with buttonholes.

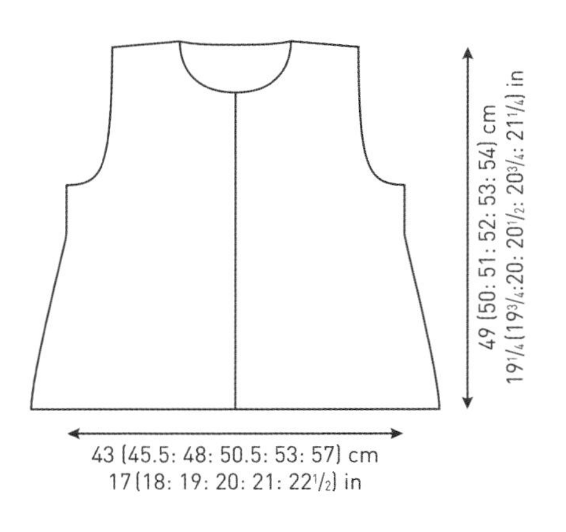

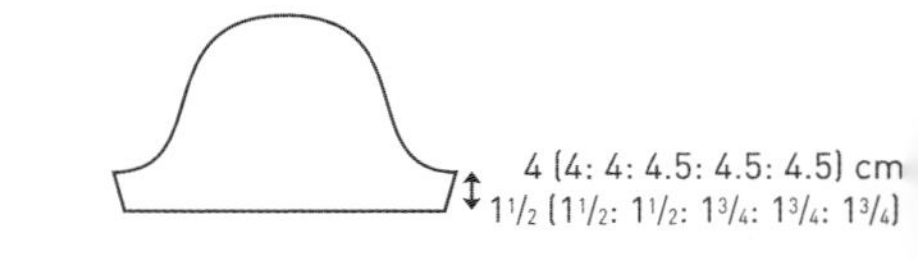

HONEY

FITTED TEXTURED JACKET WITH CABLE PANELS

Recommendation
Suitable for the more experienced knitter
Please see pages 14 & 15 for photographs.

	XS	S	M	L	XL	XXL	
To fit	**81**	**86**	**91**	**97**	**102**	**107**	**cm**
bust	32	34	36	38	40	42	in

Rowan All Seasons Cotton
Photographed in Soul

10	11	11	12	12	13	x50gm

Needles
1 pair 4 mm (no 8) (US 6) needles
1 pair 4 ½ mm (no 7) (US 7) needles
Cable needle

Button - 1

Tension
19 sts and 27 rows to 10 cm measured over textured stitch using 4 ½ mm (US 7) needles

BACK
Cast on 93 (97: 101: 105: 111: 119) sts using 4 ½ mm (US 7) needles.
Row 1 (RS): P0 (1: 0: 0: 1: 1), (K1b, P1) 6 (6: 7: 8: 8: 9) times, K6, P1, (K1b, P1) 4 times, K6, P1, (K1b, P1) 13 (14: 15: 15: 17: 19) times, K6, P1, (K1b, P1) 4 times, K6, (P1, K1b) 6 (6: 7: 8: 8: 9) times, P0 (1: 0: 0: 1: 1).
Row 2: K12 (13: 14: 16: 17: 19), P6, K9, P6, K27 (29: 31: 31: 35: 39), P6, K9, P6, K12 (13: 14: 16: 17: 19).
These 2 rows form the patt and set the stitches for the placing of the cables.
Keeping sts correct work 6 rows, ending with a WS row.
Row 9 (RS)(cable): Patt 12 (13: 14: 16: 17: 19), C6B, patt 9, C6B, patt 27 (29: 31: 31: 35: 39), C6F, patt 9, C6F, patt to end.
Row 10: Work as row 2.
Place a marker on the needle at each end of both 9 st rib panels, i.e. the 9 sts between the cables - 4 markers in total.
Row 11 (RS)(dec): *Patt to next marker, P2tog, patt to within 2 sts of next marker, P2tog tbl; rep from *, patt to end.
89 (93: 97: 101: 107: 115) sts.
Work 5 rows.
Row 17 (RS)(cable): Patt to 6 sts before marker, C6B, patt to next marker, C6B, patt to 6 sts before marker, C6F, patt to next marker, C6F, patt to end.
Work 1 row.
Row 19 (RS)(dec): P2tog, *patt to next marker, P2tog, patt to within 2 sts of next marker, P2tog tbl; rep from *, patt to last 2 sts, P2tog.
83 (87: 91: 95: 101: 109) sts.
Work 5 rows.
Row 25 (RS)(cable): Work as row 17.
Work 1 row.
Row 27 (RS)(dec): Work as row 11.
79 (83: 87: 91: 97: 105) sts.
Work 5 rows.
Row 33 (RS)(cable): Work as row 17.
Work 1 row.
Row 35 (RS)(dec): P2tog, *patt to next marker, P3tog, remove next marker; rep from *, patt to last 2 sts, P2tog.
73 (77: 81: 85: 91: 99) sts.
(There are now only 2 markers.)
Work 1 row.

Key
- K on RS, P on WS
- K1 through back loop on RS row
- P on RS, K on WS
- Slip 3 sts onto cn, hold at back, K3, K3 from cn.
- Slip 3 sts onto cn, hold at front, K3, K3 from cn.
- Slip 1 st onto cn, hold at back, K3, P1 from cn.
- Slip 3 sts onto cn, hold at front, P1, K3 from cn.

ChartB

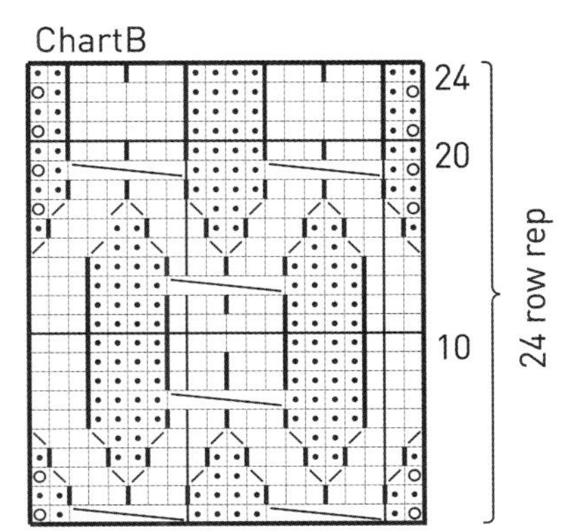

ChartA

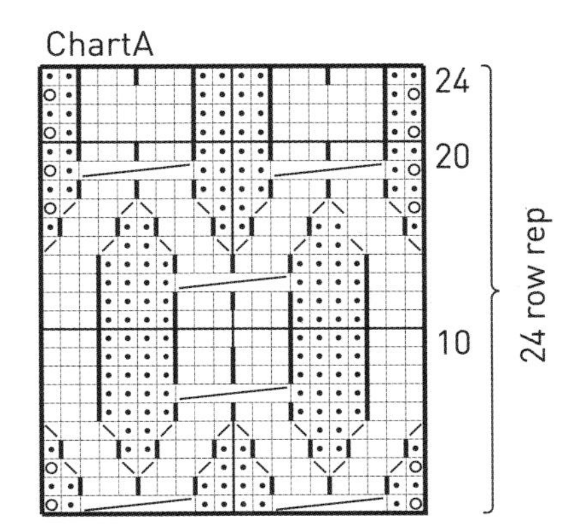

Change to 4mm (US 6) needles.
Work 8 rows twisting cables as before on the 5th of these 8 rows.
Change to 4 ½ mm (US 7) needles.
Work 2 rows, ending with a WS row.
Next row (RS)(inc): *Patt to next marker, inc in next st; rep from *, patt to end.
75 (79: 83: 87: 93: 101) sts.
Next row (WS)(inc): *patt to within 2 sts of next marker, inc in each of next 2 sts; rep from *, patt to end. 79 (83: 87: 91: 97: 105) sts.
Set sts for rib patt and cable panels as folls:
Chart row 1 (RS): Patt 8 (9: 10: 12: 13: 15), work 20 sts from **chart A** row 1, patt 23 (25: 27: 27: 31: 35), work 20 sts from **chart B** row 1, patt 8 (9: 10: 12: 13: 15).
Chart row 2: Patt 8 (9: 10: 12: 13: 15), work 20 sts from **chart B** row 2, patt 23 (25: 27: 27: 31: 35), work 20 sts from **chart A** row 2, patt 8 (9: 10: 12: 13: 15).
These 2 rows set the stitches for the cable panels.
Cont from chart, rep the 24 row patt throughout and **at the same time** shape sides as folls:
Keeping patt correct, inc 1 st at each end of next row and 6 (6: 4: 4: 4: 4) foll 6th rows and then for **M, L, XL & XXL sizes only,** 2 foll 8th rows, ending with a RS row.
93 (97: 101: 105: 111: 119) sts.
Work 11 rows.

Shape armholes

Keeping patt correct shape armholes as folls:
Cast off 4 sts at beg of next 2 rows.
85 (89: 93: 97: 103: 111) sts.
Dec 1 st at each end of next 5 (5: 7: 7: 7: 9) rows, then on 2 (3: 2: 2: 4: 4) foll alt rows, and then on foll 4th row. 69 (71: 73: 77: 79: 83) sts.
Work straight until armhole measures 16.5 (17.5: 17.5: 18.5: 19.5: 20.5) cm, ending with a WS row.

Shape back neck

Patt until there are 29 (29: 29: 31: 31: 32) sts on needle and turn, leaving rem sts on a holder.
Work each side of neck separately.
Dec 1 st at neck edge on the next 3 rows, ending with a WS row.
26 (26: 26: 28: 28: 29) sts.

Shape shoulder

Cast off 8 (8: 8: 9: 9: 9) sts at beg and dec 1 st at end of next row.
Work 1 row.
Rep last 2 rows once more.
Cast off rem 8 (8: 8: 8: 8: 9) sts.
With RS facing rejoin yarn to rem sts, cast off centre 11 (13: 15: 15: 17: 19) sts, patt to end.
Complete to match first side, reversing shaping.

Left front

Cast on 55 (56: 59: 61: 64: 68) sts using 4 ½ mm (US 7) needles.
Row 1 (RS): P0 (1: 0: 0: 1: 1), (K1b, P1) 6 (6: 7: 8: 8: 9) times, K6, P1, (K1b, P1) 4 times, K6, P1, (K1b, P1) 6 (6: 7: 7: 8: 9) times, K9.
Row 2: K22 (22: 24: 24: 26: 28), P6, K9, P6, K12 (13: 14: 16: 17: 19).
These 2 rows form the patt and set the stitches for cables, and the front band which is worked in **garter st**, i.e. knit every row.
Keeping sts correct, work 6 rows, ending with a WS row.
Row 9 (RS)(cable): Patt 12 (13: 14: 16: 17: 19), C6B, patt 9, C6B, patt 13 (13: 15: 15: 17: 19), K9.
Row 10: Work as row 2.
Place a marker on the needle at each end of 9 st rib panel, i.e. the 9 sts between the cables - 2 markers in total.
Row 11 (RS)(dec): Patt to next marker, P2tog, patt to within 2 sts of next marker, P2tog tbl, patt to end.
53 (54: 57: 59: 62: 66) sts.
Work 5 rows.
Row 17 (RS)(cable): Patt to 6 sts before marker, C6B, patt to next marker, C6B, patt to end.
Work 1 row.
Row 19 (RS)(dec): P2tog, patt to next marker, P2tog, patt to within 2 sts of next marker, P2tog tbl, patt to end.
50 (51: 54: 56: 59: 63) sts.
Work 5 rows.
Row 25 (RS)(cable): Work as row 17.
Work 1 row.
Row 27 (RS)(dec): Work as row 11.
48 (49: 52: 54: 57: 61) sts.
Work 5 rows.
Row 33 (RS)(cable): Work as row 17.
Work 1 row.
Row 35 (RS)(dec): P2tog, patt to next marker, P3tog, remove next marker, patt to end.
45 (46: 49: 51: 54: 58) sts.
Work 1 row.
Change to 4mm (US 6) needles.
Work 8 rows, placing a **button marker** and twisting cables as before on the 5th of these 8 rows.
Change to 4 ½ mm (US 7) needles.
Work 2 rows, ending with a WS row.
Next row (RS)(inc): Patt to marker, inc in next st, patt to end. 46 (47: 50: 52: 55: 59) sts.
Next row (WS)(inc): Patt to within 2 sts of marker, inc in each of next 2 sts, patt to end.
48 (49: 52: 54: 57: 61) sts.
Remove marker.
Set sts for rib patt and cable panels as folls:
Chart row 1 (RS): Patt 8 (9: 10: 12: 13: 15), work 20 sts from **chart A** row 1, patt 20 (20: 22: 22: 24: 26).
Chart row 2: Patt 20 (20: 22: 22: 24: 26), work 20 sts from **chart A** row 2, patt to end.
These 2 rows set the stitches for the cable panels.
Cont from chart, rep the 24 row patt throughout and **at the same time** shape front neck and sides as folls:
Next row (RS)(inc): Inc in first st, patt to end.
49 (50: 53: 55: 58: 62) sts.
Work 1 row.
Next row (RS)(dec): Patt to last 11 sts, P2tog tbl, K to end. 48 (49: 52: 54: 57: 61) sts.
Work 3 rows.
Next row (RS)(inc): Inc in first st, patt to end.
49 (50: 53: 55: 58: 62) sts.
Work 5 rows.
Cont shaping front edge by dec 1 st as before at front edge on next row and 7 (7: 4: 4: 2: 1) foll 10th rows and then on 0 (0: 5: 5: 8: 10) foll 8th rows and **at the same time** inc 1 st at side edge, on next row 4 (4: 2: 2: 2: 2) foll 6th rows and then for **M, L, XL & XXL sizes only,** 2 foll 8th rows, as on back, ending with a RS row.
Cont until front matches back to shape armholes, ending with a WS row.
50 (51: 54: 56: 58: 62) sts.

Shape armhole

Keeping patt and front neck shaping correct, shape armhole as folls:
Cast off 4 sts at beg of next row (working neck dec as appropriate).
Work 1 row.
Dec 1 st at armhole edge on next 5 (5: 7: 7: 7: 9) rows, then on 2 (3: 2: 2: 4: 4) foll alt rows, and then on foll 4th row.
Cont until front neck shaping completed and 34 (34: 34: 36: 36: 37) sts rem.

Work straight until front matches back to shape shoulder, ending with a WS row.

Shape shoulder

Cast off 8 (8: 8: 9: 9: 9) sts at beg of next and foll alt row.

Work 1 row.

Cast off 8 (8: 8: 8: 8: 9) sts, inc in next st, K to end. 11 sts.

Work 7.5 (7.5: 8: 8: 8.5: 8.5) cm in garter st for back neck edging.

Cast off.

Right front

Cast on 55 (56: 59: 61: 64: 68) sts using 4 ½ mm (US 7) needles.

Row 1 (RS): K9, P1, (K1b, P1) 6 (6: 7: 7: 8: 9) times, K6, P1, (K1b, P1) 4 times, K6, (P1, K1b) 6 (6: 7: 8: 8: 9) times, P0 (1: 0: 0: 1: 1).

Row 2: K12 (13: 14: 16: 17: 19), P6, K9, P6, K to end.

These 2 rows form the patt and set the stitches for cables, and the front band which is worked in **garter st,** i.e. knit every row.

Keeping sts correct, work 6 rows, ending with a WS row.

Row 9 (RS)(cable): K9, patt 13 (13: 15: 15: 17: 19), C6F, patt 9, C6F, patt to end.

Row 10: Work as row 2.

Place a marker on the needle at each end of 9 st rib panel, i.e. the 9 sts between the cables - 2 markers.

Complete as given for left front, rev cables and shaping and **at the same time** work a buttonhole to correspond with button marker as folls:

Buttonhole row (RS): K4, cast off 3, work to end.

Next row: Work across row, casting on 3 sts over those cast off on previous row.

Sleeves (both alike)

Cast on 85 (87: 89: 91: 93: 95) sts using 4 ½ mm (US 7) needles and work in rib patt setting sts as folls:

Row 1 (RS): P1, (K1b, P1) to end.

Row 2: Knit.

These 2 rows form the patt and are rep throughout.

Cont in patt, shaping sides as folls:

Work 2 rows.

Dec 1 st at each end of next row and every foll 4th row to 59 (61: 63: 65: 67: 69) sts.

Work straight until sleeve measures 23 (24: 25: 26: 27: 28) cm, ending with a WS row.

Shape sleeve top

Cast off 4 sts at beg of next 2 rows.

51 (53: 55: 57: 59: 61) sts.

Dec 1 st at each end of next 3 rows and foll alt row.

Work 3 rows.

Dec 1 st at each end of next row and every foll 4th row until 33 (35: 37: 39: 39: 39) sts rem, ending with a RS row.

Work 1 row.

Dec 1 st at each end of next row and 1 (2: 2: 3: 3: 2) foll alt rows and then every foll row to 19 (19: 21: 21: 21: 23) sts.

Cast off.

Cuff

With RS of sleeve facing, cast on edge uppermost and using 4mm (US 6) needles, pick up and knit 85 (87: 89: 91: 93: 95) sts along lower edge.

Next row (WS)(dec): P1, (P2tog) to last 2 (0: 2: 0: 2: 0) sts, P2 (0: 2: 0: 2: 0).

44 (44: 46: 46: 48: 48) sts.

Next row (RS): (K2, P2) to last 0 (0: 2: 2: 0: 0) sts, K0 (0: 2: 2: 0: 0).

Next row: P0 (0: 2: 2: 0: 0), (K2, P2) to end.

These 2 rows form the rib and are rep throughout.

Cont until cuff measures 9 (9: 9.5: 9.5: 10: 10) cm.

Cast off in rib.

Making up

Press as described on the information page.

Join the shoulder seams using back st or mattress st if preferred.

Join the side seams and sleeve seams.

Set sleeves into armholes.

With RS facing, join the cast-off ends of the back neck edging together, then neatly stitch into place around back neck.

Sew on button.

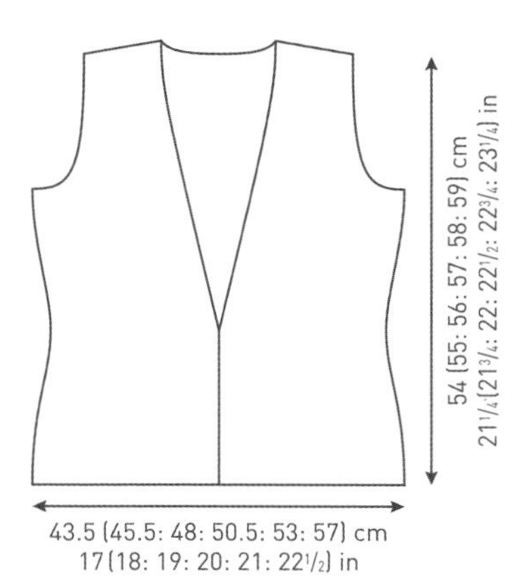

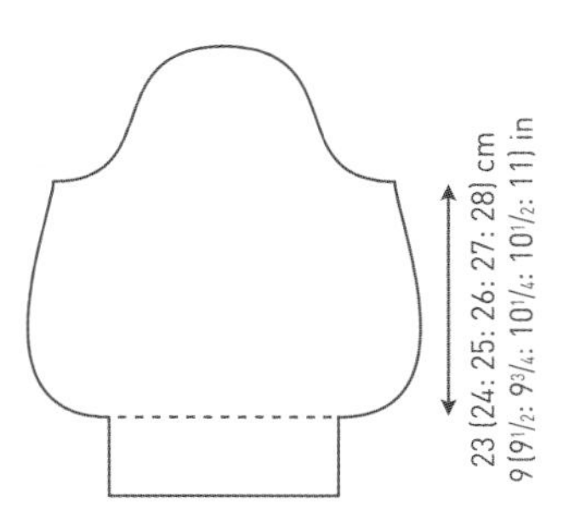

LAGOON

UNDERSTATED OPENWORK TUNIC WITH GARTER STITCH TRIM

Recommendation
Suitable for the knitter with a little experience
Please see page 10 for photograph.

	XS	S	M	L	XL	XXL	
To fit	**81**	**86**	**91**	**97**	**102**	**107**	**cm**
bust	32	34	36	38	40	42	in

Rowan Handknit Cotton
Photographed in Bleached

9	10	11	11	12	13	x50gm

Needles
1 pair 3 ¾ mm (no 9) (US 5) needles
1 pair 4mm (no 8) (US 6) needles
Cable needle

Tension
15 sts and 28 rows to 10 cm measured over pattern using 4 mm (US 6) needles.

Tension note:
The fabric of this garment is quite stretchy, so before measuring your tension pull the knitting gently into shape. The instructions are written to rows rather than length, so for the finished garment to be the correct size it is essential that the above tension is achieved.

BODY (knitted in one piece)
Starting at lower front edge:
Cast on 87 (91: 95: 101: 105: 113) sts using 3 ¾ mm (US 5) needles.
Row 1 (RS): K1, (K1, P1) to last 2 sts, K2.
Row 2: K1, (P1, K1) to end.
Rep these 2 rows until work measures 8 (8: 8: 9: 9: 9) cm, ending with a **RS** row.
Change to 4mm (US 6) needles.
Next row (WS) (dec): P2 (8: 1: 9: 1: 0), P2tog, *P3 (2: 3: 2: 3: 3), P2tog; rep from * 15 (17: 17: 19: 19: 21) times more, P to end.
70 (72: 76: 80: 84: 90) sts.
Row 1 (RS): P1, (yon, P2tog) to last st, P1.
Row 2: Work as row 1.
These 2 rows form the patt and are rep throughout.
Work 32 (32: 34: 36: 36: 36) rows, ending with a WS row.
Keeping patt correct shape sides as folls:
Next row (RS)(inc): K into front, back and front again of first st, patt to last st, K into front, back and front again of last st.
74 (76: 80: 84: 88: 94) sts.
Work 15 rows, ending with a WS row.
Inc 2 sts as before at each end of next row and foll 14th row, and then on foll 10th row, ending with a **RS** row.
86 (88: 92: 96: 100: 106) sts.
Work 7 rows.
Inc 2 sts as before at each end of next row, then on foll 6th row, and then on foll 4th row.
98 (100: 104: 108: 112: 118) sts.
Work 1 row.
Next row (RS): Cast on and K 15 sts, patt to end.
113 (115: 119: 123: 127: 133) sts.
Next row: Cast on and K 15 sts, patt to last 15 (15: 15: 17: 17: 17) sts, P1, K to end.
128 (130: 134: 138: 142: 148) sts.
Place a marker at each end of last row.
Row 1: K14 (14: 14: 16: 16: 16), (yon, P2tog) to last 14 (14: 14: 16: 16: 16) sts, K to end.
Row 2: Work as row 1.
Rep the last 2 rows until 30 (32: 32: 32: 36: 36) rows in all completed from markers, ending with a WS row.

Divide for front neck
Next row (RS): K14 (14: 14: 16: 16: 16), patt 36 (36: 38: 38: 38: 40) and turn, leaving rem sts on a holder.
50 (50: 52: 54: 54: 56) sts.
Work each side of neck separately.
Next row (WS): P2, patt to end.
Next row (RS)(dec): Patt to last 4 sts, P1, P3tog.
48 (48: 50: 52: 52: 54) sts.
Work 1 row.
Dec 2 sts as before at neck edge on next row and 4 (3: 3: 4: 1: 2) foll alt rows and then on 1 (2: 2: 2: 3: 3) foll 4th rows, ending with a **RS** row.
36 (36: 38: 38: 42: 42) sts.
Work 5 rows.
Place a marker at each end of last row to denote the shoulder line.
Shape back neck
Work 4 rows.
Next row (RS)(inc): Patt to last st, knit into front, back and front again of next st.
38 (38: 40: 40: 44: 44) sts.
Work 3 rows.
Inc 2 sts as before at neck edge on next row and 0 (1: 1: 1: 2: 2) foll 4th rows and then on 5 (4: 4: 5: 2: 3) foll alt rows, ending with a **RS** row.
50 (50: 52: 54: 54: 56) sts. ***
Leave sts on a spare needle.
With RS facing rejoin yarn to rem sts, cast off centre 28 (30: 30: 30: 34: 36) sts, patt to end.
Cont as given for first side, rev shaping, to ***, ending with a **RS** row.
Join back neck
Next row (RS): Patt right back stitches, cast on 28 (30: 30: 30: 34: 36) sts, patt across 50 (50: 52: 54: 54: 56) sts of left back.
128 (130: 134: 138: 142: 148) sts.
Work straight until back matches front from marker at shoulder to end of underarm shaping, ending with a WS row.
Shape underarm
Cast off 15 sts at the beg of the next 2 rows.
98 (100: 104: 108: 112: 118) sts.

Next row (RS)(dec): P3tog, (yon, P2tog) to last 3 sts, P3tog.
94 (96: 100: 104: 108: 114) sts.
Work 3 rows.
Dec 2 sts as before at each end of next row, then on foll 6th row, and then on foll 8th row.
82 (84: 88: 92: 96: 102) sts.
Work 9 rows.
Dec 2 sts as before at each end of next row, then on foll 14th row, and then on foll 16th row, ending with a **RS** row.
70 (72: 76: 80: 84: 90) sts.
Work 32 (32: 34: 36: 36: 36) rows, ending with a **RS** row.
Next row (WS) (inc): P2 (8: 1: 9: 1: 0), inc in next st, *P3 (2: 3: 2: 3: 3), inc in next st; rep from * 15 (17: 17: 19: 19: 21) times more, P to end.
87 (91: 95: 101: 105: 113) sts.
Change to 3 ¾ mm (US 5) needles.
Work in rib to match front.
Cast off in rib.

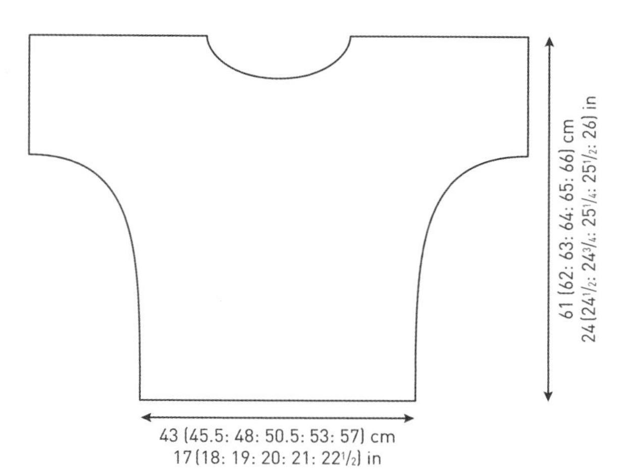

Making up
Press knitting using a warm iron over a damp cloth.
Join the side and underarm seams using back stitch or mattress st if preferred.
Neck edging
Cast on 9 (9: 9: 10: 10: 10) sts using 4mm (US 6) needles.
Work in garter st, i.e. knit every row, until edging fits around front neck from left to right shoulder marker and across back to left shoulder.
Slip stitch into place, stretching edging slightly to give a neat finish, adjusting length if necessary.
Join cast on and cast off edges of edging together.

DAWN

OPENWORK CARDIGAN WITH GARTER STITCH TRIM

Recommendation
Suitable for the knitter with a little experience
Please see pages 11 - 13 for photographs.

	XS	S	M	L	XL	XXL	
To fit	**81**	**86**	**91**	**97**	**102**	**107**	**cm**
bust	32	34	36	38	40	42	ins

Rowan Handknit Cotton
Photographed in Bleached

6	7	7	8	8	9	x100gm

Needles
1 pair 3 ¾ mm (no 9) (US 5) needles
1 pair 4mm (no 8) (US 6) needles
Cable needle

Buttons - 2

Tension
15 sts and 28 rows to 10 cm measured over pattern using 4 mm (US 6) needles.

Tension note:
The fabric of this garment is quite stretchy, so before measuring your tension pull the knitting gently into shape. The instructions are written to rows rather than length, so for the finished garment to be the correct size it is essential that the above tension is achieved.

Shrug (knitted in one piece)
Left front
Cast on 40 (42: 44: 46: 48: 50) sts using 3 ¾ mm (US 5) needles and work as folls:
Row 1 (RS): (K1, P1) to last 12 (12: 12: 14: 14: 14) sts, K12 (12: 12: 14: 14: 14).
Row 2: K12 (12: 12: 14: 14: 14), (K1, P1) to end.
Rep these 2 rows until work measures 7 (7: 7: 8: 8: 8) cm, ending with a WS row.
Change to 4mm (US 6) needles.
Row 1: P1, (yon, P2tog) to last 13 (13: 13: 15: 15: 15) sts, P1, K12 (12: 12: 14: 14: 14).
Row 2: K12 (12: 12: 14: 14: 14), P1, (yon, P2tog) to last st, P1.
Shape front neck
Row 3 (RS)(dec): P1, (yon, P2tog) to last 15 (15: 15: 17: 17: 17) sts, P3tog, K12 (12: 12: 14: 14: 14).
38 (40: 42: 44: 46: 48) sts.
Work 11 rows.
Rep last 12 rows once more.
36 (38: 40: 42: 44: 46) sts.
Dec 2 sts as before at front edge on next row and 5 foll 12th rows, **and at the same time** shape underarm as folls:
Work 6 (6: 6: 8: 8: 8) rows, ending with a WS row.
34 (36: 38: 40: 42: 44) sts.
Shape underarm
Next row (RS)(inc): K into front, back and front again of first st, work to end.
36 (38: 40: 42: 44: 46) sts.
Work 7 rows, ending with a WS row.
34 (36: 38: 40: 42: 44) sts.
Keeping front neck shaping correct, inc 2 sts as before at side edge on next row, then on foll 8th row, and then on foll 4th row.
Work 1 row.
Inc 2 sts as before at beg of next row, ending with a **RS** row.
Next row (WS)(inc): Work 1 row, turn and cast on 14 (14: 14: 16: 16: 16) sts.
54 (56: 58: 62: 64: 66) sts.
Next row (RS): K12 (12: 12: 14: 14: 14), P1, (yon, P2tog) to last 13 (13: 13: 15: 15: 15) sts, P1, K12 (12: 12: 14: 14: 14).
Working 12 (12: 12: 14: 14: 14) sts at each end of row in **garter st** i.e. K every row, and keeping front neck shaping correct, cont until the 8th front neck dec completed and 48 (50: 52: 56: 58: 60) sts rem, ending with a WS row.
Work 19 (21: 23: 27: 29: 33) rows, ending with a WS row.
Place a marker to indicate shoulder line, at end of last row.
Shape back neck
Next row (RS): Work to last 12 (12: 12: 14: 14: 14) sts and turn, leaving rem sts on a holder for back neck edging.
36 (38: 40: 42: 44: 46) sts.
Work 4 (6: 6: 6: 6: 6) rows, ending at neck edge.
Next row (WS): Cast on 2 sts, work to end.
38 (40: 42: 44: 46: 48) sts.
Work 1 row.
Rep the last 2 rows twice more, ending with a **RS** row.
42 (44: 46: 48: 50: 52) sts.
Leave sts on a spare needle.

Right front
Cast on 40 (42: 44: 46: 48: 50) sts using 3 ¾ mm (US 5) needles and work as folls:
Row 1 (RS): K12 (12: 12: 14: 14: 14), (K1, P1) to end.
Row 2: (K1, P1) to last 12 (12: 12: 14: 14: 14) sts, K12 (12: 12: 14: 14: 14).
Rep these 2 rows twice more, ending with a WS row.
Row 7 (RS)(buttonhole row): K5, cast off 3 sts, patt to end.
Row 8: Patt to end, casting on 3 sts over those cast off on previous row.
Cont until **rib** is 2 rows shorter then left front rib.
Work a second buttonhole as before on next row.
Work 1 row.
Change to 4mm (US 6) needles.

Row 1: K12 (12: 12: 14: 14: 14), P1, (yon, P2tog) to last st, P1.
Row 2: P1, (yon, P2tog) to last 13 (13: 13: 15: 15: 15) sts, P1, K12 (12: 12: 14: 14: 14).
Shape front neck
Row 3 (RS)(dec): K12 (12: 12: 14: 14: 14), P3tog tbl, (yon, P2tog) to last st, P1.
Work 11 rows.
Rep last 12 rows once more.
36 (38: 40: 42: 44: 46) sts.
Dec 2 sts as before at front edge on next row and 5 foll 12th rows, **and at the same time** shape underarm as folls:
Work 6 (6: 6: 8: 8: 8) rows, ending with a WS row.
34 (36: 38: 40: 42: 44) sts.
Shape underarm
Next row (RS)(inc): Work to last st, K into front, back and front again of last st.
36 (38: 40: 42: 44: 46) sts.
Work 7 rows, ending with a WS row.
34 (36: 38: 40: 42: 44) sts.
Keeping front neck shaping correct, inc 2 sts as before at side edge on next row, then on foll 8th row, and then on foll 4th row.
Work 1 row.
Inc 2 sts as before at end of next row, ending with a **RS** row.
Work 1 row.
Next row (RS)(inc): Work 1 row, turn and cast on 14 (14: 14: 16: 16: 16) sts.
54 (56: 58: 62: 64: 66) sts.
Working 12 (12: 12: 14: 14: 14) sts at each end of row in **garter st** i.e. K every row, and keeping front neck shaping correct, cont until the 8th front neck dec completed and 48 (50: 52: 56: 58: 60) sts rem, ending with a WS row.
Work 19 (21: 23: 27: 29: 33) rows, ending with a WS row.
Place a marker to indicate shoulder line, at beg of last row.
Shape back neck
Next row (RS): Work 12 (12: 12: 14: 14: 14) sts and leave these sts on a holder for back neck edging, work to end.
36 (38: 40: 42: 44: 46) sts.
Work 5 (7: 7: 7: 7: 7) rows ending at neck edge.
Next row (RS): Cast on 2 sts, work to end.
38 (40: 42: 44: 46: 48) sts.
Work 1 row.
Rep last 2 rows once more.
Next row (RS): Cast on 2 sts, work to end.
42 (44: 46: 48: 50: 52) sts.

Join fronts together
Next row (WS): Patt across right front sts, cast on 28 (28: 28: 32: 32: 34) sts, patt across 42 (44: 46: 48: 50: 52) sts of left front.
112 (116: 120: 128: 132: 138) sts.
Work straight until back matches fronts from marker at shoulder to end of underarm shaping, ending with a WS row.
Shape underarm
Cast off 14 (14: 14: 16: 16: 16) sts at beg of next 2 rows.
84 (88: 92: 96: 100: 106) sts.
Next row (RS)(dec): P3tog, (yon, P2tog) to last 3 sts, P3tog.
80 (84: 88: 92: 96: 102) sts.
Work 1 row.
Dec 2 sts as before at each end of next row, then on foll 4th row, and then on 2 foll 8th rows.
64 (68: 72: 76: 80: 86) sts.
Work straight until back matches fronts to top of rib.
Change to 3 ¾ mm (US 5) needles and work in K1, P1 rib until back matches fronts.
Cast off.
Making up
Press knitting using a warm iron over a damp cloth.
Join the side and underarm seam using back stitch or mattress st if preferred.
Back neck edging (work both sides the same)
Slip 12 (12: 12: 14: 14: 14) sts from holder at neck onto 4mm (US 6) needles, rejoin yarn and cont in garter st for a further 14 (14: 14: 15: 15: 15) rows.
Cast off.
With RS facing, join the cast-off ends of the neckband together, then neatly stitch into place around back neck.
Sew on buttons.

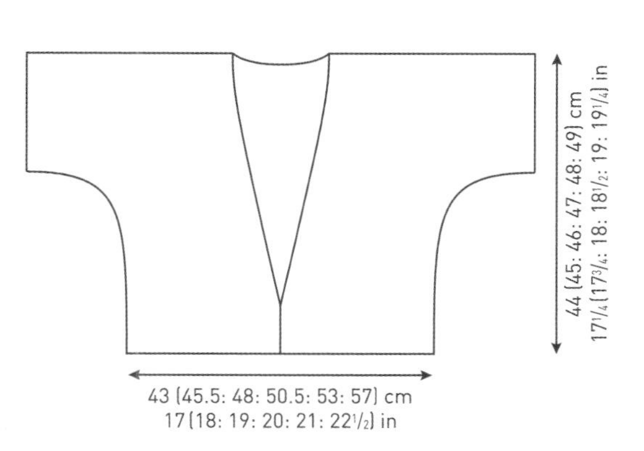

GLIMMER

DOUBLE BUTTON CARDIGAN WITH FLARED CUFF

Recommendation
Suitable for the knitter with a little experience
Please see page 16 for photograph.

	XS	S	M	L	XL	XXL	
To fit	**81**	**86**	**91**	**97**	**102**	**107**	**cm**
bust	32	34	36	38	40	42	in

Rowan Summer Tweed
Photographed in Hurricane

9	9	10	11	11	12	x50gm

Needles
1 pair 4½ mm (no 7) (US 7) needles
1 pair 5 mm (no 6) (US 8) needles

Buttons - 2

Tension
16 sts and 23 rows to 10 cm measured over reverse st st using 5 mm (US 8) needles.

Special abbreviations
MP = Make picot: cast on 2 sts, cast off 2 sts.

BACK
Peplum (knitted from side to side)
Cast on 23 (24: 25: 26: 27: 28) sts using 4½ mm (US 7) needles.
**Knit 2 rows.
Shape side edge
Next row (RS): MP, K until 8 sts on right needle, wrap next stitch, turn and K to end.
Next row: MP, K until 12 sts on right needle, wrap next stitch, turn and K to end.
Next row: MP, K until 16 sts on right needle, wrap next stitch, turn and K to end.
Next row: MP, K until 20 sts on right needle, wrap next stitch, turn and K to end.**
Keeping picot edging correct as set, cont in garter st for a further 108 (116: 124: 132: 140:148) rows, ending with a WS row.
*****Shape side edge**
Next row: MP, K until 20 sts on right needle, wrap next stitch, turn and K to end.
Next row: MP, K until 16 sts on right needle, wrap next stitch, turn and K to end.
Next row: MP, K until 12 sts on right needle, wrap next stitch, turn and K to end.
Next row: MP, K until 8 sts on right needle, wrap next stitch, turn and K to end.
Knit 2 rows. ***
Cast off, but do not break yarn.
Upper back
With RS of lower edging facing and using 5 mm (US 8) needles, pick up and knit 56 (60: 64: 68: 72: 76) sts evenly along the top (straight) edge of peplum and knit 1 row, ending with a WS row.
Beg with a P row, cont in rev st st as folls:
Work 4 rows, ending with a WS row.
Next row (RS)(inc): P2, M1P, P to last 2 sts, M1P, P2.
58 (62: 66: 70: 74: 78) sts.
Work 5 rows.
Inc as before on next row, then on every foll 6th row until there are 68 (72: 76: 80: 84: 88) sts.
Cont straight until back measures 20 (20: 21: 21: 22: 22) cm from top of peplum, ending with a WS row.
Shape armholes
Cast off 4 sts at beg of next 2 rows.
60 (64: 68: 72: 76: 80) sts.
Dec 1 st at each end of next 3 rows, then on 1 (2: 2: 2: 3: 3) foll alt rows, then on every foll 4th row until 50 (52: 56: 60: 62: 66) sts rem.
Cont straight until armhole measures 19 (20: 20: 21: 21: 22) cm, ending with a WS row.
Shape shoulders and back neck
Cast off 4 (5: 5: 6: 6: 7) sts, P until 11 (11: 13: 13: 14: 15) sts on right needle and turn, K2tog, knit to end.
Cast off 4 (5: 5: 6: 6: 7) sts at beg and dec 1 st at end of next row.
Work 1 row.
Cast off rem 5 (4: 6: 5: 6: 6) sts.
With RS facing rejoin yarn to rem sts, cast off centre 20 (20: 20: 22: 22: 22) sts, P to end.
Complete to match fi rst side, reversing shapings.

LEFT FRONT
Peplum (knitted from centre front to side seam)
Cast on 23 (24: 25: 26: 27: 28) sts using 4½ mm (US 7) needles.
Row 1 (RS): MP, K to end.
Row 2: Knit.
MP at beg of every RS row as set, cont in garter st for a further 68 (72: 76: 80: 84: 88) rows, ending with a WS row.
Work as back from *** to ***.
Cast off, but do not break yarn.
Upper left front
With RS facing, starting at side edge and using 5 mm (US 8) needles, pick up and knit 37 (39: 41: 43: 45: 47) sts evenly along the top (straight) edge of peplum, and knit 1 row, ending with a WS row.
Next row (RS): P to last 17 sts, K17.
Next row: Knit.
Last 2 rows set the sts – reverse st st with 17 st garter stitch border.
Keeping patt correct as set, work 2 rows, ending with a WS row.
Next row (inc): P2, M1P, P to last 17 sts, K17.
38 (40: 42: 44: 46: 48) sts.

Next row (short row shaping row): K16, wrap next stitch, turn and knit to end.
Work 5 rows, ending with a WS row.
Cont shaping side and front edge as folls:
Next row (inc)(dec): P2, M1P, P to last 19 sts, P2tog tbl, K17.
38 (40: 42: 44: 46: 48) sts.
Next row (short row shaping row): K16, wrap next stitch, turn and knit to end.
*Work 5 rows.
Next row (inc): P2, M1P, P to last 17 sts, K17.
39 (41: 43: 45: 47: 49) sts.
Next row (short row shaping row): K16, wrap next stitch, turn and knit to end.
Rep from * twice more, ending with a **RS** row.
41 (43: 45: 47: 49: 51) sts.
Work 1 row.
Next row (dec): P to last 19 sts, P2tog tbl, K17. 40 (42: 44: 46: 48: 50) sts.
Work 3 rows.
Next row (inc): P2, M1, P to last 17 sts, K17.
41 (43: 45: 47: 49: 51) sts.
Cont to work short row shaping on next row and every foll 6th row throughout, dec at front edge on 20th (20th: 20th: 18th: 18th: 18th) row from previous dec, and **at the same time,** when left front matches back to beg of armhole shaping, shape armhole as folls:
Shape armhole
Next row (RS): Cast off 4 sts, patt to end.
Work 1 row.
Dec 1 st at armhole edge on next 3 rows, then on foll 1 (2: 2: 2: 3: 3) foll alt rows, then on foll 4th row.
Cont to dec at front edge on every foll 20th (20th: 20th: 18th: 18th: 18th) row from previous dec until 30 (31: 33: 34: 35: 37) sts rem.
Keeping short row shaping correct, cont straight until left front matches back to start of shoulder shaping, ending with a WS row.
Shape shoulder
Cast off 4 (5: 5: 6: 6: 7) sts at beg of next and foll alt row.
Work 1 row.
Next row (RS): Cast off 5 (4: 6: 5: 6: 6) sts, inc in next st, K to end. 18 sts.
****Next row (short row shaping row):** K16, wrap next stitch, turn and knit to end.
Knit 4 rows, ending with a **RS** row.
Rep from ** 3 times more, ending with a **RS** row.

Shape edging
Knit 14 sts, wrap next stitch, turn and K to end.
Knit 10 sts, wrap next stitch, turn and K to end.
Knit 6 sts, wrap next stitch, turn and K to end.
Cast off.

RIGHT FRONT
Peplum (knitted from side seam to centre front)
Cast on 23 (24: 25: 26: 27: 28) sts using 4½ mm (US 7) needles and cont in garter stitch throughout as folls:
Work as for back from ** to **.
MP at beg of every RS row as set, cont in garter st for a further 70 (74: 78: 82: 86: 90) rows, ending with a WS row.
Cast off **purlwise,** but do not break yarn.
Upper right front With RS facing, starting at front edge and using 5 mm (US 8) needles, pick up sts along the top (straight) edge of peplum as folls:
Next row (RS) (buttonhole): Pick up and knit 4 sts, turn and cast on 3 sts, turn and leaving space for 3 sts, pick and knit 5 sts, turn and cast on 3 sts, turn and leaving space for 3 sts, pick up and knit 22 (24: 26: 28: 30: 32) sts to end.
Knit 1 row, ending with a WS row.
37 (39: 41: 43: 45: 47) sts.
Next row (RS): K17, P to end.
Next row: Knit.
Last 2 rows set the sts – reverse st st with 17 st garter stitch border.
Keeping patt correct as set, work 2 rows, ending with a WS row.
Next row (short row shaping row)(inc): K16, wrap next stitch, turn and knit to end, turn and K17, P to last 2 sts, M1P, P2.
38 (40: 42: 44: 46: 48) sts.
Work 5 rows, ending with a WS row.
Cont shaping side and front edge as folls:
Next row (short row shaping row)(inc)(dec): K16, wrap next stitch, turn and knit to end, turn and K17, P2tog, P to last 2 sts, M1P, P2.
38 (40: 42: 44: 46: 48) sts.
*Work 5 rows.
Next row (short row shaping row)(inc):: K16, wrap next stitch, turn and knit to end, turn and K17, P to last 2 sts, M1P, P2.
39 (41: 43: 45: 47: 49) sts.
Rep from * twice more, ending with a **RS** row.
41 (43: 45: 47: 49: 51) sts.
Work 1 row.

Next row (dec): K17, P2tog, P to end.
40 (42: 44: 46: 48: 50) sts.
Work 3 rows.
Next row (short row shaping row)(inc): K16, wrap next stitch, turn and knit to end, turn and K17, P to last 2 sts, M1P, P2.
41 (43: 45: 47: 49: 51) sts.
Cont to work short row shaping on next row and every foll 6th row throughout, dec at front edge on 20th (20th: 20th: 18th: 18th: 18th) row from previous dec, and **at the same time,** when right front matches back to beg of armhole shaping, ending with a **RS** row, shape armhole as folls:
Shape armhole
Next row (WS): Cast off 4 sts, patt to end.
Dec 1 st at armhole edge on next 3 rows, then on foll 1 (2: 2: 2: 3: 3) foll alt rows, then on foll 4th row.
Cont to dec at front edge on every foll 20th (20th: 20th: 18th: 18th: 18th) row from previous dec until 30 (31: 33: 34: 35: 37) sts rem.
Keeping short row shaping correct, cont straight until right front matches back to shoulder shaping, ending with a **RS** row.
Shape shoulder
Cast off 4 (5: 5: 6: 6: 7) sts at beg of next and foll alt row.
Work 1 row.
Next row (RS): Cast off 5 (4: 6: 5: 6: 6) sts, inc in next st, K to end. 18 sts.
****Next row (short row shaping row):** K16, wrap next stitch, turn and knit to end.
Knit 4 rows, ending with a WS row.
Rep from ** 3 times more, ending with a WS row.
Shape edging
Knit 14 sts, wrap next stitch, turn and K to end.
Knit 10 sts, wrap next stitch, turn and K to end.
Knit 6 sts, wrap next stitch, turn and K to end.
Cast off.

SLEEVES (both alike)
Cuff (knitted from side to side)
Cast on 10 sts using 4½ mm (US 7) needles and work in garter stitch as folls:
Knit 2 rows.
Next row (RS): MP, K to end.
Next row: Knit.
MP at beg of every RS row, cont in garter st for a further 86 (90: 94: 98: 102: 106) rows ending with a WS row.
Cast off, but do not break yarn.

Upper sleeve
With RS of cuff facing and using 5 mm (US 8) needles pick up and knit 46 (48: 50: 52: 54: 56) sts evenly along the top (straight) edge of cuff and knit 1 row, ending with a WS row.
Next row (RS) (dec): P2, P2tog, P to last 4 sts, P2tog tbl, P2.
Work 3 rows.
Dec as before on next row, then on 3 foll 4th rows.
36 (38: 40: 42: 44: 46) sts.
Work 9 rows.
Next row (RS)(inc): P2, M1P, P to last 2 sts, M1P, P2.
Work 9 rows.
Inc as before on next row, then on 1 (2: 2: 5: 5: 5) foll 10th rows, then on 4 (3: 3: 0: 0: 0) foll 8th rows.
50 (52: 54: 56: 58: 60) sts.
Cont straight until sleeve measures 44 (45: 46: 47: 48: 49) cm from lower edge, ending with a WS row.
Shape sleeve top
Cast off 4 sts at beg of next 2 rows.
42 (44: 46: 48: 50: 52) sts.
Dec 1 st at each end of next 3 rows, then on foll alt row, then on every foll 4th row until 24 (26: 28: 30: 32: 34) sts rem.
Work 1 row.
Dec 1 st at each end of next row and 0 (1: 1: 1: 1: 1) foll alt row, then on 1 (1: 1: 3: 3: 5) foll rows.
Cast off rem 20 (20: 22: 20: 22: 20) sts.

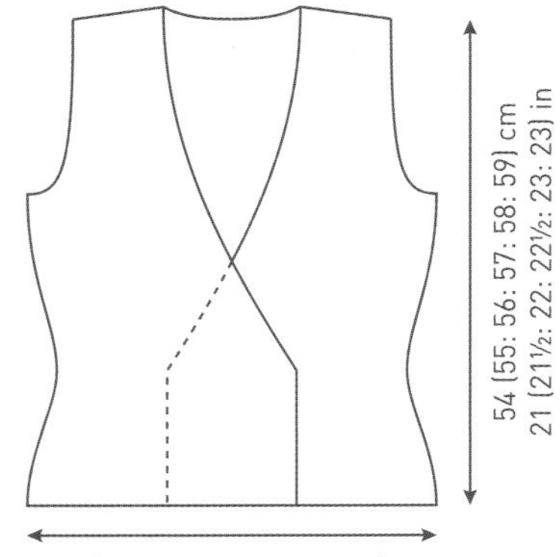

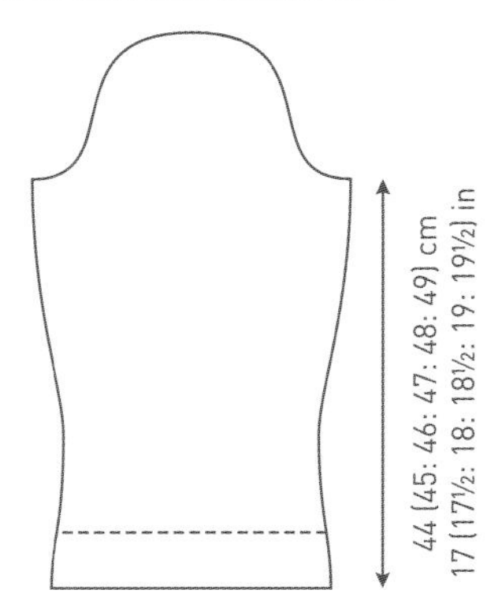

MAKING UP
Press all pieces using a warm iron over a damp cloth.
Join shoulder seams, using backstitch or mattress stitch if preferred.
Join the cast-off edges of the extended front edgings neatly together, and slipstitch neatly in place around back neck.
Join side and sleeve seams.
Set sleeves into armholes.
Sew on buttons.

BREEZE

TEXTURED LONG-LINE CARDIGAN

Recommendation
Suitable for the more experienced knitter
Please see pages 20, 40 & 41 for photographs.

	XS	S	M	L	XL	XXL	
To fit	**81**	**86**	**91**	**97**	**102**	**107**	**cm**
bust	32	34	36	38	40	42	in

Rowan Denim
Photographed in Ecru & Tennessee

19	19	20	21	22	23	x50gm

Needles
1 pair 3 ¾ mm (no 9) (US 5) needles
1 pair 4 mm (no 8) (US 6) needles

Buttons - 5

Tension
Before washing: 20 sts and 28 rows to 10 cm measured over pattern using 4 mm (US 6) needles.

Tension note:
Denim will shrink in length when washed for the first time. Allowances have been made in the pattern for shrinkage (see size diagram for after washing measurements).

BACK
Cast on 97 (101: 107: 113: 117: 123) sts using 3¾ mm (US 5) needles.
Work 24 rows in garter st, ending with a WS row.
Change to 4 mm (US 6) needles and cont in patt as folls:
Row 1 (RS): Knit.
Row 2: K6 (6: 9: 12: 6: 6), P3 (0: 0: 0: 1: 4), K7 (0: 0: 0: 7: 7), *P5, K7, rep from * to last 9 (11: 2: 5: 7: 10) sts, P3 (0: 0: 1: 4), K6 (6: 2: 5: 6: 6).
Row 3: K9 (6: 6: 6: 7: 10), P7 (0: 3: 6: 7: 7), *K5, P7, rep from * to last 9 (11: 14: 17: 7: 10) sts, K3 (5: 5: 5: 1: 4), P0 (0: 3: 6: 0: 0), K6.
Rows 4 to 7: As rows 2 and 3, twice.
Row 8: As row 2.
Row 9: Knit.
Row 10: K10 (12: 6: 6: 8: 11), P0 (0: 2: 0: 0: 0), K0 (0: 7: 0: 0: 0), *P5, K7, rep from * to last 3 (5: 8: 11: 1: 4) sts, P0 (0: 2: 5: 0: 0), K3 (5: 6: 6: 1: 4).
Row 11: K6 (6: 3: 6: 6: 6), P4 (6: 0: 0: 2: 5), *K5, P7, rep from * to last 15 (17: 8: 11: 13: 16) sts, K5 (5: 8: 11: 5: 5), P4 (6: 0: 0: 2: 5), K6 (6: 0: 0: 6: 6).
Rows 12 to 15: As rows 10 and 11, twice.
Row 16: As row 10.
These 16 rows form patt with 6 st garter stitch border.
Cont as set for a further 30 (32: 34: 36: 38: 40) rows, ending with a WS row.
Now, taking all sts into patt and omitting garter stitch border, work a further 10 (10: 10: 8: 8: 8) rows, ending with a WS row.
Shape sides
Next row (RS) (dec): Keeping patt correct, patt 2, right dec, patt to last 4 sts, left dec, patt 2. 95 (99: 105: 111: 115: 121) sts.
Work 13 rows.
Dec as before on next and foll 14th row, then on every foll 10th row until 83 (87: 93: 99: 103: 109) sts rem.
Work 27 rows straight, ending with a WS row.
Next row (RS) (inc): Keeping patt correct, patt 2, M1, patt to last 2 sts, M1, patt 2. 85 (89: 95: 101: 105: 111) sts.
Work 11 rows.
Inc as before on next row and every foll 12th row until there are 91 (95: 101: 107: 111: 117) sts, taking incs into patt.
Cont straight until work meas 79 (79: 80: 80: 81: 81) cm, ending with a WS row.
Shape armholes
Keeping patt correct, cast off 4 (4: 4: 5: 5: 5) sts at beg of next 2 rows.
83 (87: 93: 97: 101: 107) sts.
Dec 1 st at each end of next 5 (5: 7: 7: 9: 9) rows, then on 3 (4: 3: 3: 2: 3) foll alt rows, then on every foll 4th row until 65 (67: 71: 75: 77: 81) sts rem.
Cont straight until armhole meas 24 (24: 25: 26: 26: 27) cm, ending with a WS row.
Shape shoulders
Cast off 6 (6: 7: 7: 8: 8) sts at beg of next 4 rows, then 6 (7: 7: 8: 7: 9) sts at beg of foll 2 rows. 29 (29: 29: 31: 31: 31) sts.
Cast off.

LEFT FRONT
Cast on 58 (60: 63: 66: 68: 71) sts using 3¾ mm (US 5) needles.
Work 24 rows in garter st, end with a WS row.
Change to 4 mm (US 6) needles and cont in patt as folls:
Row 1 (RS): Knit.
Row 2: K13, *P5, K7, rep from * to last 9 (11: 2: 5: 7: 10) sts, P3 (0: 0: 1: 4), K6 (6: 2: 5: 6: 6).
Row 3: K9 (6: 6: 6: 7: 10), P7 (0: 3: 6: 7: 7), *K5, P7, rep from * to last 18 sts, K to end.
Rows 4 to 7: As rows 2 and 3, twice.
Row 8: As row 2.
Row 9: Knit.
Row 10: K19, *P5, K7, rep from * to last 3 (5: 8: 11: 1: 4) sts, P0 (0: 2: 5: 0: 0), K3 (5: 6: 6: 1: 4).
Row 11: K6 (6: 3: 6: 6: 6), P4 (6: 0: 0: 2: 5), *K5, P7, rep from * to last 24 sts, K5, P6, K to end.
Rows 12 to 15: As rows 10 and 11, twice.
Row 16: As row 10.
These 16 rows form patt with 13 st garter st border at front opening edge and 6 st garter stitch border to form side vent.

Cont as set for a further 30 (32: 34: 36: 38: 40) rows, ending with a WS row.
Now, taking side seam vent sts into patt, but keeping front opening edge garter stitch border correct, work a further 10 (10: 10: 8: 8: 8) rows, ending with a WS row.

Shape side seam

Next row (RS) (dec): Patt 2, right dec, patt to end. 57 (59: 62: 65: 67: 70) sts.
Work 13 rows.
Dec as before on next and foll 14th row, then on every foll 10th row until 51 (53: 56: 59: 61: 64) sts rem.
Work 27 rows straight, ending with a WS row.
Next row (RS) (inc): Patt 2, M1, patt to end. 52 (54: 57: 60: 62: 65) sts.
Work 11 rows.
Inc as before on next row and every foll 12th row until there are 55 (57: 60: 63: 65: 68) sts, taking incs into patt.
Cont straight until left front matches back to beg of armhole shaping, ending with a WS row.

Shape armhole

Keeping patt correct, cast off 4 (4: 4: 5: 5: 5) sts at beg of next row.
51 (53: 56: 58: 60: 63) sts.
Work 1 row.
Dec 1 st at armhole edge of next 5 (5: 7: 7: 9: 9) rows, then on 3 (4: 3: 3: 2: 3) foll alt rows, then on every foll 4th row until 42 (43: 45: 47: 48: 50) sts rem.
Work 5 rows straight, ending with a WS row.

Shape collar

Keeping main part of work in patt and taking extra sts into garter st for collar, work straight as folls:
Next row (RS): Patt to last 14 sts, K to end.
Next row: K14, patt to end.
Next row (RS): Patt to last 15 sts, K to end.
Next row: K15, patt to end.
Next row (RS): Patt to last 16 sts, K to end.
Next row: K16, patt to end.
Next row (RS): Patt to last 17 sts, K to end.
Next row: K17, patt to end.
Next row (RS): Patt to last 18 sts, K to end.
Next row: K18, patt to end.
Next row (RS): Patt to last 19 sts, K to end.
Next row: K19, patt to end.
Next row (RS): Patt to last 20 sts, K to end.
Next row: K20, patt to end.
Next row (RS): Patt to last 21 sts, K to end.
Next row: K21, patt to end.
Next row (RS): Patt to last 22 sts, K to end.
Next row: K22, patt to end.
Rep last 2 rows once more.
Next row (RS): Patt to last 23 sts, K to end.
Next row: K23, patt to end.
Rep last 2 rows once more.
Next row (RS): Patt to last 24 sts, K to end.
Next row: K24, patt to end.

Large and X large sizes only

Rep last 2 rows once more.
Next row (RS): Patt to last 25 sts, K to end.
Next row: K25, patt to end.

All sizes

Keeping patt correct as now set, cont straight until left front matches back to start of shoulder shaping, ending with a WS row.

Shape shoulder

Cast off 6 (6: 7: 7: 8: 8) sts at beg of next and foll alt row.
Work 1 row.
Cast off 6 (7: 7: 8: 7: 9) sts at beg of next row.
24 (24: 24: 25: 25: 25) sts.
Work 1 row, ending with a WS row.
Break yarn, leaving rem sts on a holder for collar.

Mark the positions of 5 buttons on left front, the 2nd one to come at waist level, halfway between the last dec and the first inc of the side seam shaping, the 1st to come 24 rows below the 2nd, with the 3rd, 4th and 5th buttons spaced 24 rows apart above the 2nd button.

RIGHT FRONT

Cast on 58 (60: 63: 66: 68: 71) sts using 3¾ mm (US 5) needles.
Work 24 rows in garter st, ending with a WS row.
Change to 4 mm (US 6) needles and cont in patt as folls:
Row 1 (RS): Knit.
Row 2: K6 (6: 9: 12: 6: 6), P3 (0: 0: 0: 1: 4), K7 (0: 0: 0: 7: 7), *P5, K7, rep from * to last 18 sts, P5, K to end.
Row 3: K13, *K5, P7, rep from * to last 9 (11: 14: 17: 7: 10) sts, K3 (5: 5: 5: 1: 4), P0 (0: 3: 6: 0: 0), K6.
Rows 4 to 7: As rows 2 and 3, twice.
Row 8: As row 2.
Row 9: Knit.
Row 10: K10 (12: 6: 6: 8: 11), P0 (0: 2: 0: 0: 0), K0 (0: 7: 0: 0: 0), *P5, K7, rep from * to last 12 sts, K to end.
Row 11: K13, P6, *K5, P7, rep from * to last 15 (17: 8: 11: 13: 16) sts, K5 (5: 8: 11: 5: 5), P4 (6: 0: 0: 2: 5), K6 (6: 0: 0: 6: 6).
Rows 12 to 15: As rows 10 and 11, twice.
Row 16: As row 10.
These 16 rows form patt with 13 st garter st border at front opening edge and 6 st garter stitch border to form side vent.
Cont as set for a further 30 (32: 34: 36: 38: 40) rows, ending with a WS row.
Now, taking side seam vent sts into patt, but keeping front opening edge garter stitch border correct, work a further 10 (10: 10: 8: 8: 8) rows, ending with a WS row.

Shape side seam

Next row (RS) (dec): Patt to last 4 sts, left dec, patt 2. 57 (59: 62: 65: 67: 70) sts.
Keeping patt correct as set, complete to match left front, reversing all shapings, and working buttonholes to correspond with markers as folls:
Buttonhole row (RS): K4, cast off 5, K4, patt to end.
Next row: Work to where 5 sts cast off, yrn 5 times, K4.
Next row: K4, K into back of each of the 5 loops, K4, patt to end.
On completion, **do not break yarn,** end with a RS row at the inside edge of garter st collar, and leave a ball of yarn attached to the work for collar.

SLEEVES (both alike)

Cast on 51 (53: 55: 57: 59: 61) sts using 3¾ mm (US 5) needles.
Work 24 rows in garter stitch, ending with a WS row.
Change to 4 mm (US 6) needles and cont in patt as folls:
Row 1 (RS): Knit.
Row 2: P0 (0: 0: 1: 2: 3), K5 (6: 7: 7: 7: 7), *P5, K7, rep from * to last 10 (11: 0: 1: 2: 3) sts, P5 (5: 0: 1: 2: 3), K5 (6: 0: 0: 0: 0).
Row 3: K0 (0: 0: 1: 2: 3), P5 (6: 7: 7: 7: 7), *K5, P7, rep from * to last 10 (11: 0: 1: 2: 3) sts, K5 (5: 0: 1: 2: 3), P5 (6: 0: 0: 0: 0).
Rows 4 to 7: As rows 2 and 3, twice.
Row 8: As row 2.
Row 9: Knit.
Row 10: P4 (0: 0: 0: 0: 0), K7 (0: 1: 2: 3: 4), *P5, K7, rep from * to last 4 (5: 6: 7: 8: 9) sts, P4 (5: 5: 5: 5: 5), K0 (0: 1: 2: 3: 4).

Row 11: Inc in 1st st, K3 (4: 0: 0: 0: 0), P0 (7: 0: 1: 2: 3), *K5, P7, rep from * to last 4 (5: 6: 7: 8: 9) sts, K3 (4: 5: 5: 5: 5), P0 (0: 0: 1: 2: 3), inc in last st. 53 (55: 57: 59: 61: 63) sts.
Row 12: K0 (1: 2: 3: 4: 5), *P5, K7, rep from * to last 5 (6: 7: 8: 9: 10) sts, P5, K0 (1: 2: 3: 4: 5).
Row 13: P0 (1: 2: 3: 4: 5), *K5, P7, rep from * to last 5 (6: 7: 8: 9: 10) sts, K5, P0 (1: 2: 3: 4: 5).
Rows 14 and 15: As rows 12 and 13.
Row 16: As row 12.
These 16 rows form patt and start sleeve shaping.
Cont in patt, inc 1 st at each end of 15th row, then on every foll 20th row until there are 63 (65: 67: 69: 71: 73) sts, taking inc sts into patt.
Cont straight until sleeve meas 52 (52: 52: 53: 53: 53) cm, ending with a WS row.

Shape sleeve top

Keeping patt correct, cast off 4 (4: 4: 5: 5: 5) sts at beg of next 2 rows.
55 (57: 59: 59: 61: 63) sts.
Dec 1 st at each end of next 3 rows, then on foll alt row, then on foll 4th row, then on every foll 6th row until 37 (39: 41: 41: 43: 43) sts rem.
Work 3 rows straight, ending with a WS row.
Dec 1 st at each end of next row and 2 (2: 2: 3: 3: 3) foll alt rows, then on foll 3 rows, ending with a WS row.
Cast off rem 25 (27: 29: 27: 29: 29) sts.

MAKING UP

Join both shoulder seams using back stitch or mattress stitch if preferred.

Collar

Slip 24 (24: 24: 25: 25: 25) stitches from right front holder onto a 3¾mm (US 5) needle, rejoin yarn and pick up and knit 29 (29: 29: 31: 31: 31) sts across back neck, K24 (24: 24: 25: 25: 25) sts from left front holder. 77 (77: 77: 81: 81: 81) sts.
Cont in garter st for a further 6 cm, ending with a WS of jacket/RS of collar row.
Cast off knitwise on WS of collar.
Machine wash all pieces together before completing sewing up.
Join side and sleeve seams, leaving side seams open for garter stitch borders to form side vents.
Set sleeves into armholes using the set-in method.
Sew on buttons.

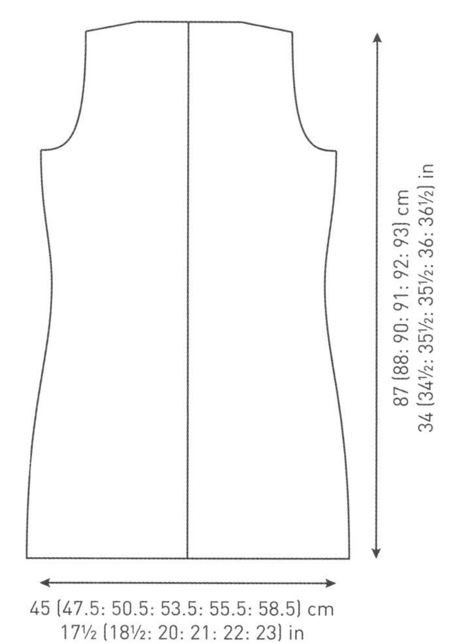

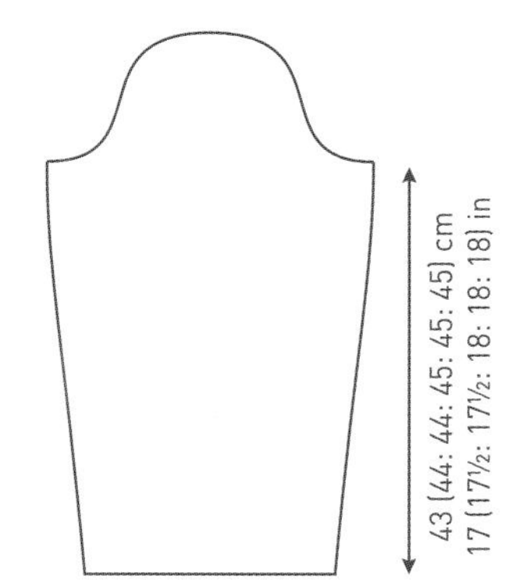

GLINT

NEAT SHRUG WITH SINGLE BUTTON

Recommendation
Suitable for the novice knitter
Please see pages 17 & 32 for photographs.

	XS	S	M	L	XL	XXL	
To fit	**81**	**86**	**91**	**97**	**102**	**107**	**cm**
bust	32	34	36	38	40	42	in

Rowan Summer Tweed
Photographed in Cotton Bud & Angel

4	5	5	6	6	7	x50gm

Needles
1 pair 4½ mm (no 7) (US 7) needles
1 pair 5 mm (no 6) (US 8) needles

Button - 1

Tension
16 sts and 23 rows to 10 cm measured over reverse stocking stitch using 5 mm (US 8) needles.

Special abbreviations
M1P = Make 1 purlwise by picking up loop before next stitch and purling into back of it.

BACK
Cast on 54 (58: 62: 66: 70: 74) sts using 4½ mm (US 7) needles.
Work in garter st for 7 rows.
Change to 5 mm (US 8) needles and, beg with a **K** row cont in rev st st as folls:
Work 1 (1: 1: 3: 3: 3) rows straight, ending with a WS row.
Next row (RS) (inc): P2, M1P, P to last 2 sts, M1P, P2.
Work 7 rows straight.
Rep last 8 rows 2 times more and then fi rst of these rows (the inc row) again.
62 (66: 70: 74: 78: 82) sts.
Cont straight until back meas 16 (16: 17: 17: 18: 18) cm, ending with a WS row.
Shape armholes
Cast off 4 sts at beg of next 2 rows.
54 (58: 62: 66: 70: 74) sts.
Dec 1 st at each end of next 1 (3: 3: 3: 3: 3) rows, then on every foll alt row until 48 (50: 54: 58: 60: 64) sts rem.
Cont straight until armhole meas 18 (19: 19: 20: 20: 21) cm, ending with a WS row.
Shape shoulders
Cast off 4 (4: 5: 5: 6: 6) sts at beg of next 4 rows, then 4 (5: 5: 6: 5: 6) sts at beg of foll 2 rows.
Leave rem 24 (24: 24: 26: 26: 28) sts on a holder.

LEFT FRONT
Cast on 31 (33: 35: 37: 39: 41) sts using 4½ mm (US 7) needles.
Work in garter st for 7 rows.
Change to 5 mm (US 8) needles and knit 1 row.
Large, X Large and XX Large sizes only
Next row (RS): P to last 2 sts, K2.
Next row: Knit.
All sizes
Next row (RS) (inc): P2, M1P, P to last 2 sts, K2.
Working 2 sts at centre front in garter st and rem sts in rev st st throughout, cont as folls:
Work 7 rows straight.
Rep last 8 rows 2 times more and then first of these rows (the inc row) again.
35 (37: 39: 41: 43: 45) sts.
Cont straight until left front matches back to beg of armhole shaping, ending with a WS row.
Shape armhole
Keeping sts correct as set, cast off 4 sts at beg of next row. 31 (33: 35: 37: 39: 41) sts.
Work 1 row.
Dec 1 st at armhole edge of next 1 (3: 3: 3: 3: 3) rows, then on every foll alt row until 28 (29: 31: 33: 34: 36) sts rem.
Cont straight until left front matches back to start of shoulder shaping, ending with a WS row.
Shape shoulder
Cast off 4 (4: 5: 5: 6: 6) sts at beg of next and foll alt row.
Work 1 row.
Cast off 4 (5: 5: 6: 5: 6) sts at beg of next row.
Work 1 row, ending with a WS row.
Break yarn, leaving rem 16 (16: 16: 17: 17: 18) sts on a holder.

RIGHT FRONT
Cast on 31 (33: 35: 37: 39: 41) sts using 4½ mm (US 7) needles.
Work in garter st for 7 rows.
Change to 5 mm (US 8) needles and knit 1 row.
Large, X Large and XX Large sizes only
Next row (RS): K2, P to end.
Next row: Knit.
All sizes
Next row (RS) (inc): K2, P to last 2 sts, M1P, P2.
Working 2 sts at centre front in garter st and rem sts in rev st st throughout, cont as folls:
Work 7 rows straight.
Rep last 8 rows once more and then first of these rows (the inc row) again.
Work 1 row, ending with a WS row.
Next row (RS) (buttonhole row): K2, P1, cast off next 3 sts, P to end.
Next row: K to end, casting-on 3 sts over those cast-off on previous row.
Next row: K2, P1, P into back of each of next 3 sts, P to end.
Work 3 rows straight.
Inc at end of next row. 35 (37: 39: 41: 43: 45) sts.
Cont straight until right front matches back to beg of armhole shaping, ending with a **RS** row.

Shape armhole
Keeping sts correct as set, cast off 4 sts at beg of next row.
31 (33: 35: 37: 39: 41) sts.
Dec 1 st at armhole edge of next 1 (3: 3: 3: 3: 3) rows, then on every foll alt row until 28 (29: 31: 33: 34: 36) sts rem.
Cont straight until right front matches back to start of shoulder shaping, ending with a **RS** row.
Shape shoulder
Cast off 4 (4: 5: 5: 6: 6) sts at beg of next and foll alt row.
Work 1 row.
Cast off 4 (5: 5: 6: 5: 6) sts at beg of next row.
Work 1 row, ending with a WS row.
Do not break yarn, leave rem 16 (16: 16: 17:17: 18) sts on a holder for neckband.

SLEEVES (both alike)
Cast on 43 (45: 47: 49: 51: 53) sts using 4½ mm (US 7) needles.
Work in garter st for 7 rows.
Change to 5 mm (US 8) needles and, beg with a K row cont in **rev st st** as folls:
Work 1 row, ending with a WS row.
Next row (RS)(inc): P2, M1P, P to last 2 sts, M1P, P2.
Work 3 (5: 5: 7: 7: 7) rows straight.
Inc as before on next row and foll 6th (6th: 6th: 6th: 8th: 8th) row.
49 (51: 53: 55: 57: 59) sts.
Cont straight until sleeve meas 10 (11: 12: 13: 14: 15) cm, ending with a WS row.
Shape top
Cast off 4 sts at beg of next 2 rows.
41 (43: 45: 47: 49: 51) sts.
Dec 1 st at each end of next 3 rows, then on foll alt row, then on every foll 4th row until 27 (29: 31: 31: 33: 35) sts rem.
Work 1 row.
Dec 1 st at each end of next and 3 (3: 3: 1: 1: 1) foll alt rows then on foll 1 (1: 1: 3: 3: 3) rows.
Cast off rem 17 (19: 21: 21: 23: 25) sts.

MAKING UP
Press all pieces using a warm iron over a damp cloth.
Join both shoulder seams using back stitch or mattress stitch if preferred.

Neck edging
With RS of right front facing and using 4½ mm (US 7) needles, work across sts from right front holder as folls: K2, P14 (14: 14: 15: 15: 16), P across 24 (24: 24: 26: 26: 28) sts from back neck holder, then work across sts from left front holder as folls: P to last 2 sts, K2.
56 (56: 56: 60: 60: 64) sts.
Knit 3 rows, ending with a WS row.
Cast off knitwise.
Join side and sleeve seams.
Set sleeve into armhole.
Sew on button.

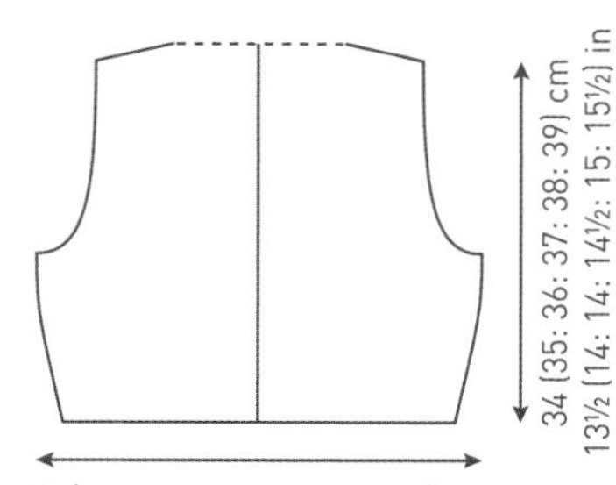

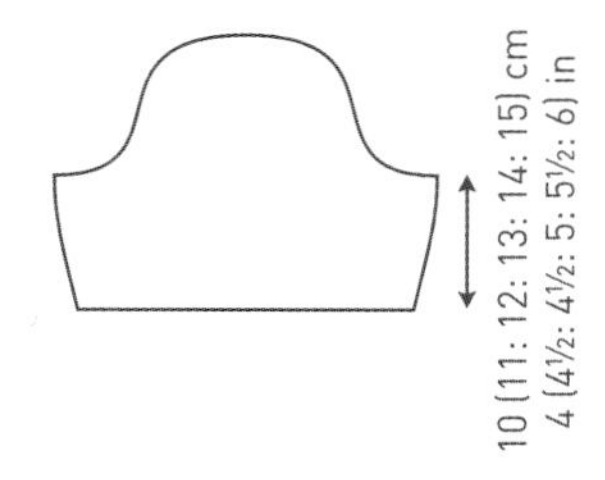

RIPPLE

CLASSIC BUTTON THROUGH SWEATER

Recommendation
Suitable for the knitter with a little experience
Please see pages 18 & 19 for photographs.

	XS	S	M	L	XL	XXL	
To fit	**81**	**86**	**91**	**97**	**102**	**109**	**cm**
bust	32	34	36	38	40	43	in

Rowan Classic Bamboo Soft
Photographed in Cream

9	10	10	11	11	12	x50gm

Needles
1 pair 3 mm (no 11) (US 2/3) needles
1 pair 3 ¼ mm (no 10) (US 3) needles
1 pair 3 ¾ mm (no 9) (US 5) needles

Buttons - 8

Tension
Before steaming: 24 sts and 30 rows to 10 cm measured over stocking stitch using 3 ¾ mm (US 5) needles.

Tension note:
The Bamboo Soft yarn relaxes after steaming; this opens the knitting and changes the tension by approximately one stitch in the width, but does not affect the rows (23 sts and 30 rows). Allowances have been made within the pattern for this change (see size diagram for after relaxing measurements).

Ridge pattern:
Row 1 (RS): Purl.
Row 2: Knit.
Rows 3 & 5: Knit.
Rows 4 & 6: Purl.
Rows 7 & 8: Knit.
Rows 9 & 10: Purl.
Row 11 & 13: Knit.
Row 12: Purl.
Row 14: Purl.
These 14 rows form the pattern.

Front edging pattern:
Row 1 (RS): Purl.
Rows 2 - 8: Knit.
Rows 9 - 14: Purl.
These 14 rows form the pattern.

Front
Cast on 96 (102: 108: 114: 120: 130) sts using 3 ¼ mm (US 3) needles and work rib setting sts as folls:
Row 1 (RS): K1 (1: 1: 1: 1: 0), (P1, K2) to last 2 (2: 2: 2: 2: 1) sts, P1, K1 (1: 1: 1: 1: 0).
Row 2: P1 (1: 1: 1: 1: 0), (K1, P2) to last 2 (2: 2: 2: 2: 1) sts, K1, P1 (1: 1: 1: 1: 0).
These 2 rows form the rib.
Rep these 2 rows until 10 (10: 12: 12: 12: 12) rows in all completed, ending with a WS row.
Keeping rib correct, dec 1 st at each end of next row.
94 (100: 106: 112: 118: 128) sts.
Work 5 more rows in rib, ending with a WS row. **
Change to 3 ¾ mm (US 5) needles and beg with a K row cont in st st, shaping sides as folls:
Next row (RS) (dec): K2, K2tog, K to last 4 sts, K2tog tbl, K2.
92 (98: 104: 110: 116: 126) sts.
Work 5 rows, ending with a WS row.
Dec 1 st as before at each end of next row and 1 (1: 1: 1: 2: 2) foll 6th rows.
88 (94: 100: 106: 110: 120) sts.
Work 1 (1: 3: 3: 1: 1) rows, ending with a WS row.
Cont shaping sides, working centre 52 (52: 58: 58: 64: 64) sts in **ridge pattern** beg with patt row 1, and setting sts as folls:
Next row (RS): K18 (21: 21: 24: 23: 28), place a marker on the needle, P52 (52: 58: 58: 64: 64) (row 1 of **ridge pattern**), place a marker on the needle, K to end.
Next row: P to first marker, slip marker from left to right needle, K to second marker (row 2 of **ridge pattern**), slip marker from left to right needle, P to end.
Working centre 52 (52: 58: 58: 64: 64) sts between markers in **ridge pattern**, cont shaping sides as folls:
Keeping sts and **ridge pattern** correct and taking the marker up the knitting as before, work 2 (2: 0: 0: 2: 2) rows, ending with a WS row.
Dec 1 st as before at each end of next row and 1 (1: 1: 1: 0: 0) foll 6th row, ending with a **RS** row.
84 (90: 96: 102: 108: 118) sts.
Work 1 (1: 3: 3: 7: 7) rows, ending with **patt row 12** (WS row) of the **ridge pattern.**
Divide for front neck
Next row (RS): Patt 39 (42: 45: 48: 51: 56), and leave these on a holder for left front, patt to end.
45 (48: 51: 54: 57: 62) sts.
Work each side of neck separately.
Work 1 row, ending with **patt row 14 of ridge pattern.**
Cont in patt but now work the 6 sts at centre front in the **front edging patt** to form buttonhole band and place the buttonholes as folls:
Keeping ridge patt correct and starting with **row 1 of front edging patt,** cont as folls:
Row 1 (RS): Purl to marker, K to end.
Row 2: Purl to marker, K to end.
Row 3: Knit.
Row 4: P to last 6 sts, K to end.
Row 5 (RS)(buttonhole row): K2, K2tog tbl, yon, K to end.
Row 6: Work as row 4.
Row 7: Work as row 3.
Row 8: Work as row 2.
Row 9: Work as row 1.
Rows 10 & 12: Purl.
Rows 11 & 13: P6, K to end.

Row 14: Purl.
These 14 rows form the patt, set the stitches for the **ridge** and **front edging patt,** and the positioning of the buttonholes.
Cont in patt on sts as set, working 6 more buttonholes, as before, on every patt row 5, and **at the same time** shape sides and armhole as folls:
Next row (RS) (inc): Patt to last 2 sts, M1, K2.
46 (49: 52: 55: 58: 63) sts.
Work 5 rows.
Inc as before on next row and 1 (1: 2: 2: 4: 4) foll 6th rows and then on 4 (4: 3: 3: 1: 1) foll 8th rows, ending with a **RS** row.
52 (55: 58: 61: 64: 69) sts.
Work 10 rows, ending with a **RS** row.
Shape armhole
Keeping patt and buttonholes correct work as folls:
Next row (WS): Cast off 4 (4: 4: 5: 5: 5) sts at beg of next row. 48 (51: 54: 56: 59: 64) sts.
Dec 1 st at armhole edge on next 5 (7: 7: 7: 7: 11) rows, then on 3 (2: 3: 3: 4: 3) foll alt rows, and then on foll 4th row.
39 (41: 43: 45: 47: 49) sts.
Cont in patt until the 7th buttonhole row completed, ending with a **RS** row.
Work 11 rows, ending with a WS row.
Shape front neck
Next row (RS): K13 (14: 13: 14: 14: 15), and leave these on a holder for neck edging, patt to end.
26 (27: 30: 31: 33: 34) sts.
Dec 1 st at neck edge on next 6 (6: 8: 8: 8: 8) rows, then on 2 (2: 2: 2: 3: 3) foll alt rows.
18 (19: 20: 21: 22: 23) sts.
Work 3 rows.
Dec 1 st at neck edge on next row and foll 4th row.
16 (17: 18: 19: 20: 21) sts.
Work straight until armhole measures 18 (19: 19: 20: 21: 22) cm, ending with a **RS** row.
Shape shoulder
Cast off 6 (6: 6: 7: 7: 7) sts at beg of next row and 5 (6: 6: 6: 7: 7) sts at beg of foll alt row.
Work 1 row.
Cast off rem 5 (5: 6: 6: 6: 7) sts.
With **WS** facing, rejoin yarn to 39 (42: 45: 48: 51: 56) sts on holder for left front and work as folls:
Cast on 6 sts, patt to end.
45 (48: 51: 54: 57: 62) sts.
Complete to match first side, reversing all shapings and omitting buttonholes.

Back
Work as given for front to **.
Change to 3 ¾ mm (US 5) needles and beg with a K row cont in **st st** throughout, shaping sides as folls:
Next row (RS) (dec): K2, K2tog, K to last 4 sts, K2 tog tbl, K2.
92 (98: 104: 110: 116: 126) sts.
Work 5 rows, ending with a WS row.
Dec 1 st as before at each end of next row and 3 foll 6th rows.
84 (90: 96: 102: 108: 118) sts.
Work 17 (17: 19: 19: 23: 23) rows straight, ending with a WS row.
Next row (RS)(inc): K2, M1, K to last 2 sts, M1, K2.
86 (92: 98: 104: 110: 120) sts.
Work 5 rows.
Inc 1 st as before at each end of next row, then on 1 (1: 2: 2: 4: 4) foll 6 th rows and then on 4 (4: 3: 3: 1: 1) foll 8th rows.
98 (104: 110: 116: 122: 132) sts.
Work 9 rows straight, ending with a WS row.
Shape armholes
Cast off 4 (4: 4: 5: 5: 5) sts at beg of next 2 rows.
90 (96: 102: 106: 112: 122) sts.
Dec 1 st at each end of next 5 (7: 7: 7: 7: 11) rows, then on 3 (2: 3: 3: 4: 3) foll alt rows, and then on foll 4th row.
72 (76: 80: 84: 88: 92) sts.
Work straight until back matches front to shoulder shaping, ending with a WS row.
Shape shoulders and back neck
Cast off 6 (6: 6: 7: 7: 7) sts at beg of next 2 rows.
Cast off 5 (6: 6: 6: 7: 7) sts, work until there are 9 (9: 10: 10: 10: 11) sts on right needle and turn, leaving rem sts on a holder.
Work each side of neck separately.
Cast off 4 sts, work to end.
Cast off rem 5 (5: 6: 6: 6: 7) sts.
With RS facing rejoin yarn to rem sts, cast off centre 32 (34: 36: 38: 40: 42) sts, work to end.
Complete to match first side, reversing shapings.

Sleeves (both alike)
Cast on 48 (50: 52: 54: 56: 58) sts using 3 ¼ mm (US 3) needles and work lower rib setting sts as folls:
Row 1 (RS): K1 (2: 0: 1: 2: 0), (P1, K2) to last 2 (0: 1: 2: 0: 1) sts, P1 (0: 1: 1: 0: 1), K1 (0: 0: 1: 0: 0).
Row 2: P1 (2: 0: 1: 2: 0), (K1, P2) to last 2 (0: 1: 2: 0: 1) sts, K1 (0: 1: 1: 0: 1), P1 (0: 0: 1: 0: 0).
These 2 row form the rib.
Rep the last 2 rows until 22 rows in all completed, ending with a WS row.
Keeping rib correct inc 1 st at each end of next row. 50 (52: 54: 56: 58: 60) sts.
Work 7 (7: 7: 9: 9: 9) more rows in rib.
Change to 3 ¾ mm (US 5) needles and cont in st st, shaping sides as folls:
Beg with a K row, work 4 (4: 4: 2: 2: 2) rows in st st.
Next row (RS)(inc): K2, M1, K to last 2 sts, M1, K2. 52 (54: 56: 58: 60: 62) sts.
Work 11 rows.
Inc 1 st as before at each end of next row and 0 (0: 0: 2: 4: 4) foll 12th rows and then on every foll 10th row to 70 (72: 74: 76: 78: 80) sts.
Work straight until sleeve measures 45 (46: 47: 48: 49: 50) cm, ending with a WS row.
Shape top
Cast off 4 (4: 4: 5: 5: 5) sts at beg of next 2 rows. 62 (64: 66: 66: 68: 70) sts.
Dec 1 st at each end of next 3 rows and foll alt row, and then on every foll 4th row to 44 (46: 48: 46: 48: 48) sts, ending with a **RS** row.
Work 1 row.
Dec 1 st at each end of next row and 2 (3: 3: 2: 3: 2) foll alt rows and then every foll row to 28 (28: 30: 30: 30: 32) sts, ending with a WS row.
Cast off 3 sts at beg of next 2 rows.
Cast off rem 22 (22: 24: 24: 24: 26) sts.

Making up
Pin the pieces out, and **steam** gently without allowing the iron to touch the yarn.
Join both shoulder seams using back stitch or mattress st if preferred.
Neck edging
With RS of right front facing and using 3 mm (US 2/3) needles, slip 13 (14: 13: 14: 14: 15) sts from holder onto right needle, rejoin yarn and pick up and knit 26 (27: 28: 29: 30: 31) sts up right front neck, 40 (42: 44: 46: 48: 50) sts across back neck and 26 (27: 28: 29: 30: 31) sts down left front neck, knit across 13 (14: 13: 14: 14: 15) sts from holder on left front.
118 (124: 126: 132: 136: 142) sts.
Knit 1 row (WS).

Next row (RS) (buttonhole row): P2, P2tog, yon, P to end.
Beg with a K row, work 4 more rows in rev st st.
Cast off knitwise (on WS).
Join side and sleeve seams.
Set sleeves into armholes.
Sew cast-on edge at base of left front opening in place behind right front opening edge.
Sew on buttons.

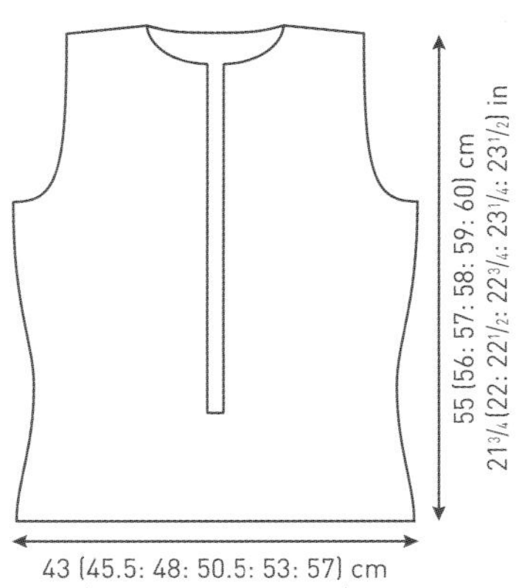

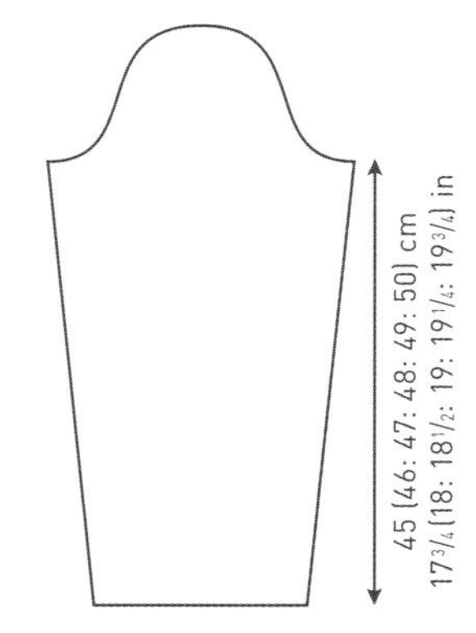

HARMONY

GARTER STITCH CARDIGAN WITH LACE PEPLUM

Recommendation

Suitable for the more experienced knitter

Please see page 21 for photograph.

	XS	S	M	L	XL	XXL	
To fit	**81**	**86**	**91**	**97**	**102**	**107**	**cm**
bust	32	34	36	38	40	42	in

Rowan Summer Tweed

Photographed in Cotton Bud

9	9	10	10	11	11	x50gm

Needles

1 pair 4½ mm (no 7) (US 7) needles

Buttons - 5

Tension

18 sts and 30 rows to 10 cm measured over garter stitch using 4½ mm (US 7) needles. Remember, garter stitch is very elastic, so a larger piece will open up and stretch in length. It is, therefore, very important that you pull the knitting slightly before measuring your knitted square in order to get an accurate tension.

Edging

Cast on 17 sts using 4½mm (US 7) needles.

Row 1 (RS): K6, (yrn, K2tog) 3 times, yrn, K2, (yrn) twice, K2tog, K1. 19 sts.

Row 2: K3, P1, K15.

Row 3: K7, (yrn, K2tog) 3 times, yrn, K6. 20 sts.

Row 4: Knit.

Row 5: K8, (yrn, K2tog) 3 times, yrn, K2, (yrn) twice, K2tog, (yrn) twice, K2. 24 sts.

Row 6: K3, P1, K2, P1, K17.

Row 7: K9, (yrn, K2tog) 3 times, yrn, K9. 25 sts.

Row 8: Knit.

Row 9: K10, [(yrn, K2tog) 3 times, yrn, K2, (yrn) twice, K2tog] 3 times, K1. 29 sts.

Row 10: K3, P1, (K2, P1) twice, K19.

Row 11: K11, (yrn, K2tog) 3 times, yrn, K12. 30 sts.

Row 12: Cast off 7 sts (1 st left on needle), to end. 23 sts.

Row 13: K12, (yrn, K2tog) 3 times, yrn, K2, (yrn) twice, K2tog, K1. 25 sts.

Row 14: K3, P1, K21.

Row 15: K13, (yrn, K2tog) 3 times, yrn, K6. 26 sts.

Row 16: Knit.

Row 17: K14, (yrn, K2tog) 3 times, yrn, K2, (yrn) twice, K2tog, (yrn) twice, K2. 30 sts.

Row 18: K3, P1, K2, P1, K23.

Row 19: Knit.

Row 20: K8, K2tog, (yrn, K2tog) 4 times, K12. 29 sts.

Row 21: K22, [(yrn) twice, K2tog] 3 times, K1. 32 sts.

Row 22: K3, P1, (K2, P1) twice, K1, K2tog, (yrn, K2tog) 4 times, K11. 31 sts.

Row 23: Knit.

Row 24: Cast off 7 (1 st left on needle), K3, K2tog, (yrn, K2tog) 4 times, K10. 23 sts.

Row 25: K20, (yrn) twice, K2tog, K1. 24 sts.

Row 26: K3, P1, K1, K2tog, (yrn, K2tog) 4 times, K9. 23 sts.

Row 27: Knit.

Row 28: K5, K2tog, (yrn, K2tog) 4 times, K8. 22 sts.

Row 29: K18, (yrn) twice, K2tog, (yrn) twice, K2. 25 sts.

Row 30: K3, P1, K2, P1, K1, K2tog, (yrn, K2tog) 4 times, K7. 24 sts.

Row 31: Knit.

Row 32: K8, K2tog, [(yrn, K2tog), 4 times, K6. 23 sts.

Row 33: K16, (yrn) twice, K2tog] 3 times, K1. 26 sts.

Row 34: K3, P1, (K2, P1) twice, K1, K2tog, (yrn, K2tog) 4 times, K5. 25 sts.

Row 35: Knit.

Row 36: Cast off 7 (1 st left on needle), K3, K2tog, K12. 17 sts.

These 36 rows form patt.

BACK AND FRONT (knitted in one piece to armholes)

Cast on 17 sts using 4½ mm (US 7) needles.

Work 6 (6: 6: 7: 7: 7) repeats of edging patt as given above.

Cast off.

Place markers on straight edge of border between 57th & 58th (57th & 58th: 57th & 58th: 65th & 66th: 65th & 66th: 65th & 66th) rows in from both ends of work.

With RS facing and using 4½ mm (US 7) needles, pick up and knit 35 (37: 39: 41: 43: 45) sts for right front from cast-on edge of edging to first marker, place marker on needle for side seam, pick up and knit 63 (67: 71: 75: 79: 83) sts from first marker to second marker for back, place marker on needle for side seam, then pick up and knit 35 (37: 39: 41: 43: 45) sts for left front from second marker to cast-off edge of edging.

133 (141: 149: 157: 165: 173) sts.

Cont in garter stitch as folls:

Next row (WS): (K to marker, slip marker from left to right needle) twice, K to end (take the marker up the knitting in this way on every row).

Next row (RS) (buttonhole): K3, cast off 3, K to end.

Next row: K to cast-off sts, yrn 3 times, K3.

Next row: K3, K into back of each of next 3 loops, K to end.

Work 5 (5: 5: 7: 7: 7) rows.

Next row (inc): * K to 2 sts before marker, M1,K4, M1, rep from *, K to end.
137 (145: 153: 161: 169: 177) sts.
Work 9 (9: 9: 11: 11: 11) rows, ending with a WS row.
Inc as before on next row.
141 (149: 157: 165: 173: 181) sts.
Work 5 (5: 5: 3: 3: 3) rows, ending with a WS row.
Next row (RS) (buttonhole): K3, cast off 3, K to end.
Next row: K to cast-off sts, yrn 3 times, K3.
Next row: K3, K into back of each of next 3 loops, K to end.
Work 1 (1: 1: 3: 3: 3) rows, ending with a WS row.
** Inc as before on next row.
145 (153: 161: 169: 177: 185) sts.
Work 9 rows.
Rep from ** once more.
149 (157: 165: 173: 181: 189) sts.
Next row (inc) (buttonhole): K3, cast off 3, (K to 2 sts before marker, M1, K4, M1) twice, K to end. 153 (161: 169: 177: 185: 193) sts.
Next row: K to cast-off sts, yrn 3 times, K3.
Next row: K3, K into back of each of next 3 loops, K to end.
Work 9 (9: 11: 9: 13: 13) rows ending with a WS row.
Divide for fronts
Next row (RS): K37 (39: 41: 43: 45: 47) sts and turn, leaving rem sts on a holder.
Knit 1 row, ending with a WS row.
Work on these 37 (39: 41: 43: 45: 47) sts for right front as folls:
Shape armhole
Dec 1 st at armhole edge on next 3 rows, then on 2 (3: 3: 3: 4: 4) foll alt rows, then on every foll 4th row until 31 (32: 34: 36: 37: 39) sts rem, and **at the same time** make a buttonhole on 24th (24th: 24th: 26th: 26th: 26th) row from previous buttonhole, ending with a **RS** row.
Work 19 (21: 19: 25: 19: 21) rows, ending with a WS row.
Next row (RS) (buttonhole): K3, cast off 3, K to end.
Next row: K to cast-off sts, yrn 3 times, K3.
Next row: K3, K into back of each of next 3 loops, K to end.
Work 1 (1: 3: 1: 1: 3) rows, ending with a WS row.
Shape front neck
Next row (RS): K12 and leave these 12 sts on a holder for neck edging, K2tog, K to end.
18 (19: 21: 23: 24: 26) sts.
Dec 1 st at neck edge on next 6 (6: 6: 8: 8: 8) rows, then every foll alt row until 10 (10: 12: 13: 14: 15) sts rem.
Cont straight until armhole meas 18 (19: 19: 20: 20: 21) cm, ending with a WS row.
Shape shoulder
Cast off 3 (3: 4: 4: 5: 5) sts at beg of next and foll alt row.
Work 1 row. Cast off rem 4 (4: 4: 5: 4: 5) sts.

Back
With RS facing rejoin yarn to sts from holder, cast off 6 sts, K until there are 67 (71: 75: 79: 83: 87) sts on right needle and turn, leaving rem sts on a holder.
Knit 1 row, ending with a WS row.
Work on these 67 (71: 75: 79: 83: 87) sts for back as folls:
Shape armholes
Dec 1 st at each end of next 3 rows, then on 2 (3: 3: 3: 4: 4) foll alt rows, then on every foll 4th row until 55 (57: 61: 65: 67: 71) sts rem.
Cont straight until 1 row less has been worked than on right front to start of shoulder shaping, ending with a WS row.
Shape shoulders and back neck
Cast off 3 (3: 4: 4: 5: 5) sts at beg of next 2 rows.
49 (51: 53: 57: 57: 61) sts.
Cast off 3 (3: 4: 4: 5: 5) sts, K until there are 8 (8: 8: 9: 8: 9) sts on right needle and turn, leaving rem sts on a holder for left front.
Work each side of neck separately.
Cast off 4 sts at beg of next row.
Cast off rem 4 (4: 4: 5: 4: 5) sts.
With RS facing rejoin yarn to rem sts, cast off 27 (29: 29: 31: 31: 33) sts, K to end.
Complete to match fi rst side, reversing shapings.

Left front
With RS facing rejoin yarn to rem sts, cast off 6 sts, K to end. 37 (39: 41: 43: 45: 47) sts.
Work 1 row, ending with a WS row.
Shape armhole
Dec 1 st at armhole edge on next 3 rows, then on 2 (3: 3: 4: 4: 4) foll alt rows, then on every foll 4th row until 31 (32: 34: 36: 37: 39) sts rem.
Work 22 (24: 24: 28: 22: 26) rows, ending with a **RS** row.
Shape front neck
Next row (WS): K12 and leave these 12 sts on a holder for neck edging, K to end.
Dec 1 st at neck edge on next 7 (7: 7: 9: 9: 9) rows, then on every foll alt row until 10 (10: 12: 13: 14: 15) sts rem.
Cont straight until left front matches back to start of shoulder shaping, ending with a WS row.
Shape shoulder
Cast off 3 (3: 4: 4: 5: 5) sts at beg of next and foll alt row.
Work 1 row.
Cast off rem 4 (4: 4: 5: 4: 5) sts.

SLEEVES (both alike)
Cast on 41 (43: 45: 47: 49: 51) using $4\frac{1}{2}$ mm (US 7) needles and cont in garter st as folls:
Knit 12 rows.
Next row (RS) (inc): K2, M1, K to last 2 sts, M1, K2. 43 (45: 47: 49: 51: 53) sts.
Working all incs as set by last row, inc 1 st at each end of every foll 12th row until there are 45 (47: 53: 57: 63: 65) sts, then on every foll 10th row until there are 57 (59: 61: 63: 65: 67) sts.
Cont straight until sleeve meas 31 (32: 33: 34: 35: 36) cm, ending with a WS row.
Shape top
Cast off 4 sts at beg of next 2 rows.
49 (51: 53: 55: 57: 59) sts.
Dec 1 st at each end of next 3 rows, and then on foll alt row, then on every foll 4th row until 37 (41: 43: 45: 47: 47) sts rem.
Work 5 rows.
Dec 1 st at each end of next row, then on 1 (2: 2: 3: 3: 3) foll 6th rows, then on every foll 4th row until 29 (31: 33: 35: 37: 37) sts rem.
Work 1 row, ending with a WS row.
Dec 1 st at each end of next row, then on 0 (0: 0: 1: 1: 1) foll alt row, then on 3 foll rows.
Cast off rem 21 (23: 25: 25: 27: 27) sts.

MAKING UP
Do not press.
Steam all pieces using a warm iron over a damp cloth.
Join both shoulder seams using backstitch or mattress stitch if preferred.

Neck edging
With RS of right front facing and using 4½ mm (US 7) needles, slip 12 stitches from right front holder onto right needle, rejoin yarn and pick up and knit 21 (21: 21: 21: 23: 23) sts up right side of neck, 35 (37: 37: 39: 39: 41) sts from back, then 21 (21: 21: 21: 23: 23) sts down left side of neck to holder, K across sts from holder. 101 (103: 103: 105: 109: 111) sts.
Knit 4 rows.
Cast off knitwise (on WS).
Join sleeve seams.
Set sleeves into armholes.
Sew on buttons.

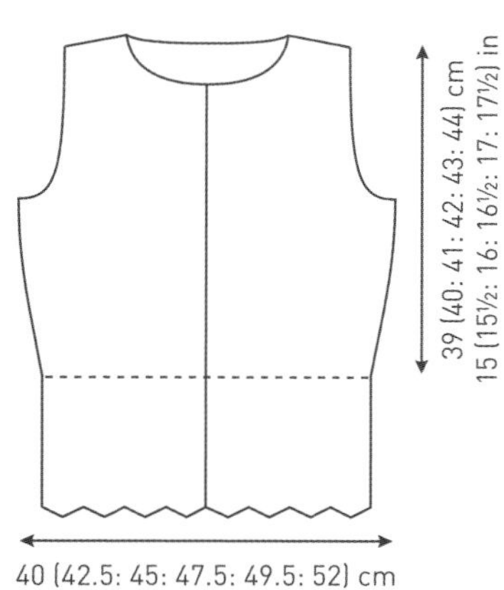

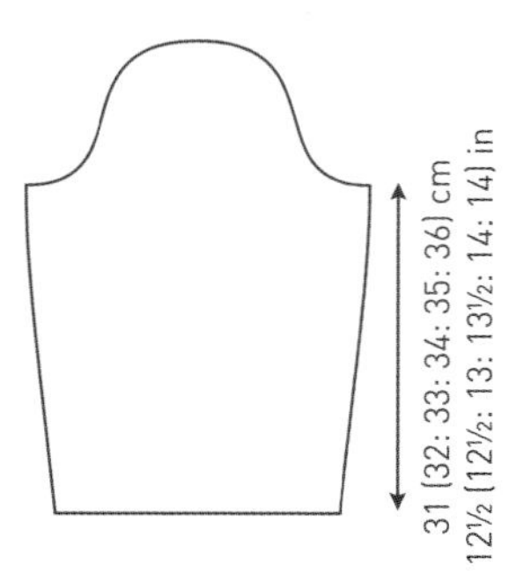

FAVOUR

A-LINE CARDIGAN WITH CABLES & FULL SLEEVES

Recommendation
Suitable for the knitter with a little experience
Please see pages 24 & 25 for photographs.

	XS	S	M	L	XL	XXL	
To fit	**81**	**86**	**91**	**97**	**102**	**107**	**cm**
bust	32	34	36	38	40	42	in

Rowan Denim
Photographed in Tennessee

18	19	19	20	20	21	x50gm

Needles
1 pair 3 ¼ mm (no 10) (US 3) needles
1 pair 4 mm (no 8) (US 6) needles
Cable needle

Buttons · 7

Tension
Before washing: 22 sts and 31 rows to 10 cm measured over textured stitch using 4 mm (US 6) needles.

Tension note:
Denim will shrink in length when washed for the first time. Allowances have been made in the pattern for shrinkage (see size diagram for after washing measurements).

BACK
Cast on 157 (163: 169: 175: 179: 189) sts using 4 mm (US 6) needles and work lower edging setting stitches as folls:
Row 1 (RS): P1 (0: 0: 0: 1: 0), (K1b, P1) to last 0 (1: 1: 1: 0: 1) st, (K1b) 0 (1: 1: 1: 0: 1) times.
Row 2: Knit.
These 2 rows form the textured rib st.
Rep these 2 rows once more.
Row 5: Patt 19 (20: 22: 24: 25: 28),* K7, patt 5, K7, patt 7, K7, patt 5, K7 *, patt 29 (33: 35: 37: 39: 43), rep from * to * once more, patt 19 (20: 22: 24: 25: 28).
Row 6: Patt 19 (20: 22: 24: 25: 28), * P7, patt 5, P7, patt 7, P7, patt 5, P7 *, patt 29 (33: 35: 37: 39: 43), rep from * to * once more, patt 19 (20: 22: 24: 25: 28).
Rep these 2 rows twice more.
Row 11: Patt 19 (20: 22: 24: 25: 28),* K7, P5, K7, P7, K7, P5, K7 *, patt 29 (33: 35: 37: 39: 43), rep from * to * once more, patt 19 (20: 22: 24: 25: 28).
Row 12: Patt 19 (20: 22: 24: 25: 28), * P7, K5, P7, K7, P7, K5, P7 *, patt 29 (33: 35: 37: 39: 43), rep from * to * once more, patt 19 (20: 22: 24: 25: 28).
These 2 rows set the stitches for the rest of the lower back.
Keeping sts correct cont in patt and shape sides as folls:
Work 20 (20: 24: 24: 24: 24) rows, ending with a WS row.
Dec 1 st at each end of next row and 2 foll 32nd rows, ending with a RS row.
151 (157: 163: 169: 173: 183) sts.
Work straight until back measures 41 (41: 42.5: 42.5: 42.5: 42.5) cm, ending with a **RS** row.
Next row (WS)(dec): P2tog, patt until 15 (16: 18: 20: 21: 24) sts on right needle, *P2tog tbl, P1, (P2tog) twice, K2tog tbl, K1, K2tog, P2tog tbl, P1, (P2tog) twice, K2tog tbl, K1, (K2tog) twice, P2tog tbl, P1, (P2tog) twice, K2tog tbl, K1, K2tog, P2tog tbl, P1, (P2tog) twice *, patt 29 (33: 35: 37: 39: 43), rep from * to * once more, patt to last 2 sts, patt 2tog.
111 (117: 123: 129: 133: 143) sts.
Place a marker at each end of last row.
Cont in patt working cable panels from charts as folls:
Next row (RS): Patt 15 (16: 18: 20: 21: 24), work next 26 sts as patt row 1 of **chart A**, patt 29 (33: 35: 37: 39: 43), work next 26 sts as patt row 1 of **chart B**, patt 15 (16: 18: 20: 21: 24).
Next row: Patt 15 (16: 18: 20: 21: 24), work next 26 sts as patt row 2 of **chart B**, patt 29 (33: 35: 37: 39: 43), work next 26 sts as patt row 2 of **chart A,** patt 15 (16: 18: 20: 21: 24).
These 2 rows set the stitches for the cable panels.
Cont from chart rep the 24 row rep throughout, as folls:
Keeping patt correct, work straight until work measures 11 cm from markers, ending with a WS row.
Shape armholes
Cast off 4 sts at beg of next 2 rows.
103 (109: 115: 121: 125: 135) sts.
Dec 1 st at each end of next 3 (5: 5: 5: 5: 7) rows, then on 4 (3: 4: 5: 5: 6) foll alt rows, and then on 2 foll 4th rows.
85 (89: 93: 97: 101: 105) sts.
Work straight until armhole measures 21 (22: 22: 23: 24.5: 25.5) cm, ending with a WS row.
Shape shoulders and back neck
Taking 2 sts together over cables, cast off 10 (10: 10: 10: 11: 11) sts at beg of next 2 rows.
Cast off 9 (9: 10: 10: 10: 10) sts, work until 13 (13: 13: 14: 14: 14) sts on right needle and turn, leaving rem sts on a holder.
Work each side of neck separately.
Cast off 4 sts, patt to end.
Cast off rem 9 (9: 9: 10: 10: 10) sts.
With RS facing rejoin yarn to rem sts, cast off centre 21 (25: 27: 29: 31: 35) sts, patt to end.
Complete to match first side reversing shapings.

Left front
Cast on 87 (90: 93: 95: 98: 103) sts using 4 mm (US 6) needles and work lower edging, setting stitches as folls:
Row 1 (RS): P1 (0: 0: 0: 1: 0), (K1b, P1) to last 6 (6: 7: 7: 7: 7) sts, (K1, P1) 3 times, K0 (0: 1: 1: 1: 1).
Row 2: K0 (0: 1: 1: 1: 1), (P1, K1) 3 times, K to end.
These 2 rows set the sts for the textured rib patt and the front edging, worked in moss st on the 6 (6: 7: 7: 7: 7) sts at the centre front.
Rep these 2 rows once more.
Row 5: Patt 19 (20: 22: 24: 25: 28), K7, patt 5, K7, patt 7, K7, patt 5, K7, patt 17 (19: 19: 19: 21: 23), moss st to end.
Row 6: Moss st 6 (6: 7: 7: 7: 7), patt 17 (19: 19: 19: 21: 23), P7, patt 5, P7, patt 7, P7, patt 5, P7, patt 19 (20: 22: 24: 25: 28).
Rep these 2 rows twice more.
Row 11: Patt 19 (20: 22: 24: 25: 28), K7, P5, K7, P7, K7, P5, K7, patt 17 (19: 19: 19: 21: 23), moss st to end.
Row 12: Moss st 6 (6: 7: 7: 7: 7), patt 17 (19: 19: 19: 21: 23), P7, K5, P7, K7, P7, K5, P7, patt 19 (20: 22: 24: 25: 28).
These 2 rows set the stitches for the rest of the lower left front.
Keeping sts correct cont in patt and shape side as folls:
Work 20 (20: 24: 24: 24: 24) rows, ending with a WS row.
Dec 1 st at beg of next row and 2 foll 32nd rows, ending with a RS row.
84 (87: 90: 92: 95: 100) sts.
Work straight until left front matches back to marked row, ending with a **RS** row.
Next row (WS)(dec): Work until 23 (25: 26: 26: 28: 30) sts on right needle, P2tog tbl, P1, (P2tog) twice, K2tog tbl, K1, K2tog, P2tog tbl, P1, (P2tog) twice, K2tog tbl, K1, (K2tog) twice, P2tog tbl, P1, (P2tog) twice, K2tog tbl, K1, K2tog, P2tog tbl, P1, (P2tog) twice, patt to last 2 sts, patt 2tog.
64 (67: 70: 72: 75: 80) sts.
Cont in patt working cable panels from charts as folls:
Next row (RS): Patt 15 (16: 18: 20: 21: 24), work next 26 sts as patt row 1 of **chart A,** patt to end.
Next row: Patt 23 (25: 26: 26: 28: 30), work next 26 sts as patt row 2 of **chart A,** patt to end.
These 2 rows set the stitches for the cable panels.
Cont from chart rep the 24 row rep throughout, as folls:
Keeping patt correct, work straight until left front matches back to beg of armhole shaping, ending with a WS row.
Shape armhole
Cast off 4 sts at beg of next row.
60 (63: 66: 68: 71: 76) sts.
Work 1 row.
Dec 1 st at armhole edge on next 3 (5: 5: 5: 5: 7) rows, then on 4 (3: 4: 5: 5: 6) foll alt rows, and then on 2 foll 4th rows.
51 (53: 55: 56: 59: 61) sts.
Work straight until front is 26 (28: 30: 32: 32: 34) rows shorter than back to shape shoulder, ending with a WS row.
Shape front neck
Next row (RS): Patt to last 11 (11: 11: 11: 12: 13) sts, turn and leave rem sts on a holder for neck edging.
40 (42: 44: 45: 47: 48) sts.
Dec 1 st at neck edge on next 6 (8: 8: 8: 10: 10) rows and 4 (4: 5: 4: 3: 4) foll alt rows, and then on 2 (2: 2: 3: 3: 3) foll 4th rows.
28 (28: 29: 30: 31: 31) sts.
Work straight until front matches back to shoulder shaping, ending with a WS row.
Shape shoulder
Taking 2 sts together over cables, cast off 10 (10: 10: 10: 11: 11) sts at beg of next row and 9 (9: 10: 10: 10: 10) sts at beg of foll alt row.
Work 1 row.
Cast off rem 9 (9: 9: 10: 10: 10) sts.
Mark position of 7 buttons, the first to come opposite first row of cables, the 7th on last row before front neck shaping and rem spaced evenly between.

Right front
Cast on 87 (90: 93: 95: 98: 103) sts using 4 mm (US 6) needles and work lower edging, setting stitches as folls:
Row 1 (RS): K0 (0: 1: 1: 1: 1), (P1, K1) 3 times, (P1, K1b) to last 1 (0: 0: 0: 1: 0) st, P1 (0: 0: 0: 1: 0).
Row 2: K to last 6 (6: 7: 7: 7: 7) sts, (K1, P1) 3 times, K0 (0: 1: 1: 1: 1).
These 2 rows set the sts for the textured rib patt and the front edging, worked in moss st on the 6 (6: 7: 7: 7: 7) sts at the centre front.
Rep these 2 rows once more.
Row 5: Moss st 6 (6: 7: 7: 7: 7), patt 17 (19: 19: 19: 21: 23), K7, patt 5, K7, patt 7, K7, patt 5, K7, patt 19 (20: 22: 24: 25: 28).
Row 6: Patt 19 (20: 22: 24: 25: 28), P7, patt 5, P7, patt 7, P7, patt 5, P7, patt 17 (19: 19: 19: 21: 23), moss st to end.
Rep these 2 rows twice more.

ChartB

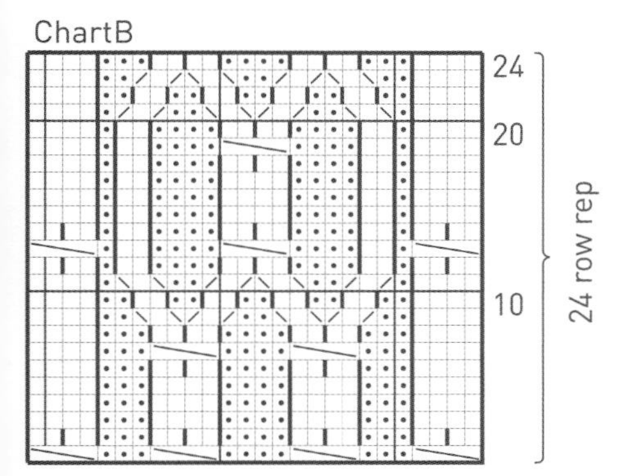

ChartA

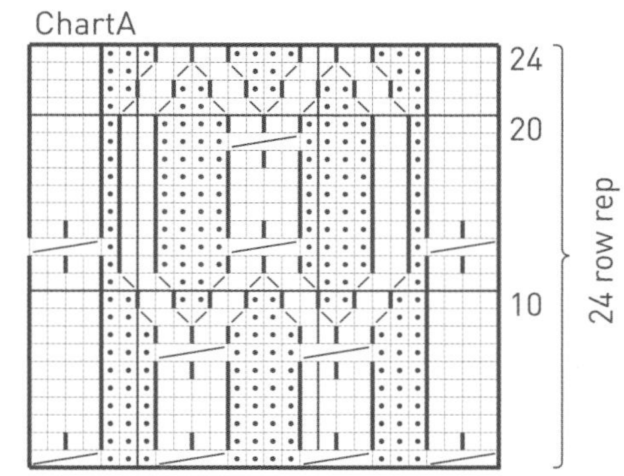

Key
- K on RS, P on WS
- P on RS, K on WS
- Slip 2 sts onto cn, hold at back, K2, K2 from cn.
- Slip 2 sts onto cn, hold at front, K2, K2 from cn.
- Slip 1 st onto cn, hold at back, K2, P1 from cn.
- Slip 2 sts onto cn, hold at front, P1, K2 from cn.

Row 11: Moss st 6 (6: 7: 7: 7: 7), patt 17 (19: 19: 19: 21: 23), K7, P5, K7, P7, K7, P5, K7, patt 19 (20: 22: 24: 25: 28).
Row 12: Patt 19 (20: 22: 24: 25: 28), P7, K5, P7, K7, P7, K5, P7, patt 17 (19: 19: 19: 21: 23), moss st to end.
These 2 rows set the stitches for the rest of the lower back.
Complete as given for left front, rev all shaping, working from **chart B** for cable pattern and working buttonholes to correspond with button markers as folls:
Buttonhole row (RS): Patt 4, yon, patt 2tog, patt to end.

Sleeves (both alike)
Cast on 91 (93: 95: 97: 99: 101) sts using 4 mm (US 6) needles and work in rib patt setting sts as folls:
Row 1 (RS): P1, (K1b, P1) to end.
Row 2: Knit.
These 2 rows form the patt and are rep throughout.
Cont in patt shaping sides as folls:
Work 4 (4: 4: 6: 6: 6) rows.
XS, S & M sizes only
Dec 1 st at each end of next row and 6 foll 6th rows, then on 3 foll 8th rows. 71 (73: 75) sts.
Work 11 rows.
Dec 1 st at each end of next row and foll 16th row. 67 (69: 71) sts.
L, XL & XXL sizes only
Dec 1 st at each end of next row and 9 foll 8th rows, then on foll 12th row, and then on foll 16th row. 73 (75: 77) sts.
All sizes
Work straight until sleeve measures 38.5 (39.5: 41: 42: 43: 44) cm, ending with a WS row.
Shape sleeve top
Cast off 4 sts at beg of next 2 rows.
59 (61: 63: 65: 67: 69) sts.
Dec 1 st at each end of next 3 rows and foll alt row.
Work 3 rows.
Dec 1 st at each end of next row and every foll 6th row to 43 (43: 45: 47: 47: 49) sts and then on 1 (1: 1: 2: 2: 3) foll 4th rows.
41 (41: 43: 43: 43: 43) sts.
Work 1 row, ending with a WS row.
Dec 1 st at each end of next row and 4 (3: 3: 3: 2: 2) foll alt rows and then on every foll row until 25 (27: 29: 29: 31: 31) sts rem.
Cast off.

Cuff
With RS of sleeve facing, cast on edge uppermost and using 3 ¼ mm (US 3) needles, pick up and knit 92 (92: 92: 100: 100: 100) sts along lower edge.
Next row (WS)(dec): (P2tog) to end. 46 (46: 46: 50: 50: 50) sts.
Next row (RS): (K2, P2) to last 2 sts, K2.
Next row: (P2, K2) to last 2 sts, P2.
These 2 rows form the rib and are rep throughout.
Cont until cuff measures 10.5 (10.5: 11: 11: 11.5: 11.5) cm.
Cast off in rib.

MAKING UP
Join shoulder seams, using back stitch or mattress st if preferred.
Neck edging
With RS of right front facing and using 3 ¼ mm (US 3) needles, slip 11 (11: 11: 11: 12: 13) sts on holder onto the right needle, pick up and knit 18 (20: 20: 22: 22: 24) sts up right front neck, 29 (33: 35: 37: 39: 43) sts across back and 18 (20: 20: 22: 22: 24) sts down left front, patt 11 (11: 11: 12: 12: 13) sts on holder.
87 (95: 97: 103: 107: 117) sts.
Keeping moss st correct, work 8 rows in moss st, ending with a **RS** row.
Cast off in patt.
Join side and sleeve seams (but do not sew sleeve into armhole until after washing).
Machine wash all pieces together before completing sewing-up.
Set sleeves into armholes.
Sew on buttons to correspond with buttonholes.

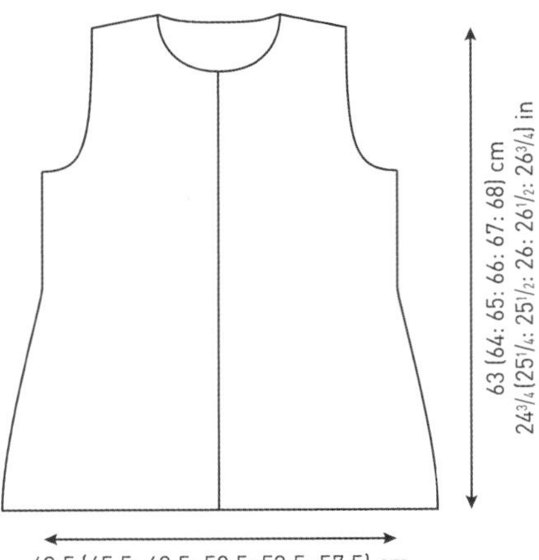

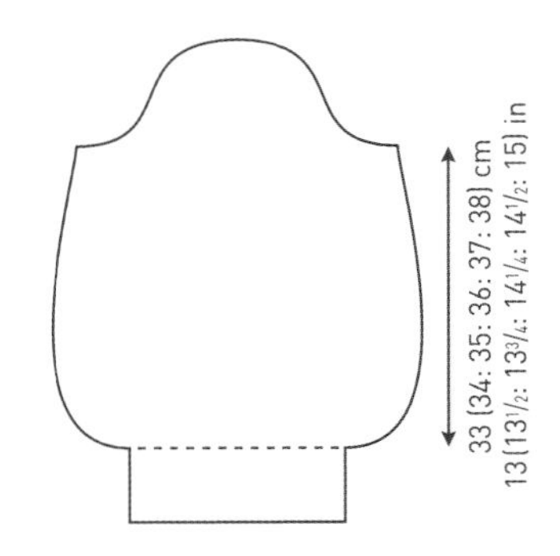

GLEE

FITTED TEXTURED CARDIGAN WITH GARTER STITCH PEPLUM

Recommendation
Suitable for the more experienced knitter
Please see pages 26 & 27 for photographs.

	XS	S	M	L	XL	XXL	
To fit	**81**	**86**	**91**	**97**	**102**	**107**	**cm**
bust	32	34	36	38	40	42	in

Rowan Denim
Photographed in Nashville

11	12	12	13	14	14	x50gm

Needles
1 pair 3¼ mm (no 10) (US 3) needles
1 pair 4 mm (no 8) (US 6) needles

Button -1

Tension
Before washing: 22 sts and 27 rows to 10 cm measured over reversed stitch using 4 mm (US 6) needles.

Tension note:
Denim will shrink in length when washed for the first time. Allowances have been made in the pattern for shrinkage (see size diagram for after washing measurements).

Special abbreviations
Cluster 3 = P3tog, but leave sts on LH needle, yrn, P3tog same 3 sts.
M1P = Make picot: cast-on 2 sts, cast-off 2 sts.

BACK
Peplum (knitted from side to side)
Cast on 27 (28: 29: 30: 31: 32) sts using 3¼ mm (US 3) needles.
Knit 2 rows.
Shape side edge
Next row (RS): MP, K until 8 sts on right needle, wrap next stitch, turn and K to end.
Next row: MP, K until 16 sts on right needle, wrap next stitch, turn and K to end.
Next row: MP, K until 20 sts on right needle, wrap next stitch, turn and K to end.
Next row: MP, K until 24 sts on right needle, wrap next stitch, turn and K to end.
Next row: MP, K until 26 (27: 28: 29: 30: 31) sts on right needle, wrap next stitch, turn and K to end.
Keeping picot edging correct as set, cont in garter st for a further 154 (162: 174: 182: 194: 202) rows, ending with a WS row.
Shape side edge
Next row: MP, K until 26 (27: 28: 29: 30: 31) sts on right needle, wrap next stitch, turn and K to end.
Next row: MP, K until 24 sts on right needle, wrap next stitch, turn and K to end.
Next row: MP, K until 20 sts on right needle, wrap next stitch, turn and K to end.
Next row: MP, K until 16 sts on right needle, wrap next stitch, turn and K to end.
Next row: MP, K until 12 sts on right needle, wrap next stitch, turn and K to end.
Next row: MP, K until 8 sts on right needle, wrap next stitch, turn and K to end.
Knit 2 rows. Cast off, but do not break yarn.
Upper back
With RS of lower edging facing and using 4 mm (US 6) needles, pick up and knit 77 (83: 89: 93: 99: 105) sts evenly along the top (straight) edge of peplum and purl 1 row, ending with a WS row.
Cont in patt as folls:
Rows 1, 3, 5 and 7: Knit.
Row 2: P1 (4: 1: 3: 6: 3), (cluster 3, P3) to last 4 (1: 4: 0: 3: 0) sts, (cluster 3) 1 (0: 1: 0: 0: 0) times, P1 (1: 1: 0: 3: 0).
Rows 4: Purl.
Row 6: P4 (1: 4: 6: 3: 6), (cluster 3, P3) to last 1 (4: 1: 3: 0: 3) sts, (cluster 3) 0 (1: 0: 0: 0: 0) times, P1 (1: 1: 3: 0: 3).
Row 8: Purl.
These 8 rows form patt and are repeated throughout.
(**NB:** Do not work any cluster less than 1 st away from edge.)
Next row (RS) (inc): K2, M1, K to last 2 sts, M1, K2.
79 (85: 91: 95: 101: 107) sts.
Working all incs as set by last row, cont in patt, inc 1 st at each end of 1 (1: 1: 2: 2: 2) foll 10th rows, then on every foll 8th row until there are 89 (95: 101: 105: 111: 117) sts, taking inc sts into patt.
Work 9 (9: 13: 11: 13: 17) rows straight, ending with a WS row.
(Work should meas approx 35 (35: 37: 37.5: 38.5: 40) cm.)
Shape armholes
Cast off 4 sts at beg of next 2 rows.
81 (87: 93: 97: 103: 109) sts.
Dec 1 st at each end of next 5 (5: 5: 5: 7: 7) rows, then on 1 (2: 3: 3: 3: 4) foll alt rows, then on every foll 4th row until 67 (71: 75: 79: 81: 85) sts rem.
Work 43 (45: 43: 47: 45: 45) rows straight, ending with a WS row.
(Armhole should meas approx 21 (22: 22: 23.5: 23.5: 24.5) cm.)
Shape shoulders and back neck
Cast off 6 (7: 7: 8: 8: 9) sts at beg of next 2 rows.
55 (57: 61: 63: 65: 67) sts.
Next row (RS): Cast off 6 (7: 7: 8: 8: 9) sts, K until there are 10 (10: 12: 11: 12: 12) sts on right needle and turn, leaving rem sts on a holder.
Work each side of neck separately.
Cast off 4 sts, patt to end.
Cast off rem 6 (6: 8: 7: 8: 8) sts.
With RS facing, rejoin yarn to rem sts, cast off centre 23 (23: 23: 25: 25: 25) sts, K to end.
Complete to match fi rst side, reversing shapings.

LEFT FRONT

Peplum (knitted from side seam to centre)

Cast on 27 (28: 29: 30: 31: 32) sts using 3 ¼ mm (US 3) needles and work in garter stitch as folls:

Next row (RS): Knit.

Next row: MP, K to end.

Next row: Knit.

Shape side edge

Next row (WS): MP, K until 8 sts on right needle, wrap next stitch, turn and K to end.

Next row: MP, K until 12 sts on right needle, wrap next stitch, turn and K to end.

Next row: MP, K until 16 sts on right needle, wrap next stitch, turn and K to end.

Next row: MP, K until 20 sts on right needle, wrap next stitch, turn and K to end.

Next row: MP, K until 24 sts on right needle, wrap next stitch, turn and K to end.

Next row: MP, K until 25 (26: 27: 28: 29: 30) sts on right needle, wrap next stitch, turn and K to end.

Working a picot at beg of every WS row, cont for a further 27 (31: 35: 37: 41: 45) rows, ending with a WS row.

Shape front edge

Next row (RS): K to last 3 sts, K2tog tbl, K1.

Working all decs as set by last row, and keeping picot edging correct as set, cont as folls:

Work 9 rows straight, ending with a WS row.

Dec at end of next row, then on foll 8th row, then on foll 6th row and then foll 4th row.

22 (23: 24: 25: 26: 27) sts.

Work 1 row.

Dec as before on next row and every foll alt row until 11 sts rem.

Next row (WS): MP, K2tog tbl, K to end.

Working decs as set, dec on every row until 6 sts rem.

Next row (RS): K2, K3tog tbl, K1.

Next row: MP, K3tog tbl.

Cast off 2 rem sts.

Upper left front

With RS of work facing, starting at side edge and using 4 mm (US 6) needles, pick up and knit 45 (48: 51: 53: 56: 59) sts evenly along the top (straight) edge of peplum and work in patt as folls:

Row 1(WS): MP, K until 10 sts on right needle, P to end.

Rows 2, 4 and 6: Knit.

Row 3: MP, K until 10 sts on right needle, P1, (cluster 3, P3) to last 4 (1: 4: 0: 3: 0) sts, (cluster 3) 1 (0: 1: 0: 0: 0) times, P1 (1: 1: 0: 3: 0).

Row 5: MP, K until 10 sts on right needle, P to end.

Row 7: MP, K until 10 sts on right needle, P4, (cluster 3, P3) to last 1 (4: 1: 3: 0: 3) sts, (cluster 3) 0 (1: 0: 0: 0: 0) times, P1 (1: 1: 3: 0: 3).

Row 8: Knit.

These 8 rows form patt and are repeated throughout.

Cont in patt as set, remembering not to work any cluster less than 1 st away from side edges.

Work 1 row straight, ending with a WS row.

Next row (RS) (inc): K2, M1, K to end.

46 (49: 52: 54: 57: 60) sts.

Work 9 rows straight, ending with a WS row.

Next row (RS) (inc): K2, M1, K to end.

47 (50: 53: 55: 58: 61) sts.

Work 7 (7: 7: 9: 9: 9) rows straight, ending with a WS row.

Next row (RS): K2, M1, K to last 12 sts, K2tog tbl, K to end.

Work 7 rows.

Rep last 8 rows 3 times more, ending with a WS row.

Next row (RS) (dec): K to last 12 sts, K2tog tbl, K to end.

46 (49: 52: 54: 57: 60) sts.

Work 1 (1: 5: 3: 5: 9) rows straight, ending with a WS row. (Left front should now match back to beg of armhole shaping.)

Shape armhole

Keeping patt correct, dec as before at neck edge on 8th row from previous dec, then on 6 (6: 6: 7: 7: 7) foll 8th rows, and **at the same time** shape armhole as folls:

Cast off 4 sts at beg of next row.

Work 1 row.

Dec 1 st at armhole edge of next 5 (5: 5: 5: 7: 7) rows, then on 1 (2: 3: 3: 3: 4) foll alt rows, then on foll 4th row.

28 (30: 32: 33: 34: 36) sts.

Work 3 (5: 9: 3: 5: 7) rows straight, ending with a WS row. (Left front should now match back to start of shoulder shaping.)

Shape shoulder

Cast off 6 (7: 7: 8: 8: 9) sts at beg of next row and foll alt row.

Work 1 row.

Cast off 6 (6: 8: 7: 8: 8) sts, K to end.

Next row (WS): MP, knit to end, inc 1 st at end of row. 11 sts.

Keeping picot edging correct as set, cont in garter stitch for a further 24 rows.

Cast off.

RIGHT FRONT

Peplum (knitted from side seam to centre)

Cast on 27 (28: 29: 30: 31: 32) sts using 3¼ mm (US 3) needles and work in garter stitch as folls:

Knit 2 rows, ending with a WS row.

Shape side edge

Next row (RS): MP, K until 8 sts on right needle, wrap next stitch, turn and K to end.

Next row: MP, K until 12 sts on right needle, wrap next stitch, turn and K to end.

Next row: MP, K until 16 sts on right needle, wrap next stitch, turn and K to end.

Next row: MP, K until 20 sts on right needle, wrap next stitch, turn and K to end.

Next row: MP, K until 24 sts on right needle, wrap next stitch, turn and K to end.

Next row: MP, K until 25 (26: 27: 28: 29: 30) sts on right needle, wrap next stitch, turn and K to end.

Working a picot at beg of every WS row, cont for a further 28 (32: 36: 38: 42: 46) rows, ending with a WS row.

Shape front edge

Next row (RS): MP, K2tog, K to end.

Working all decs as set by last row, and keeping picot edging correct as set, cont as folls:

Work 9 rows straight, ending with a WS row.

Dec at beg of next row, then on foll 8th row, then on foll 6th row and then foll 4th row.

22 (23: 24: 25: 26: 27) sts.

Work 1 row.

Dec as before on next row and every foll alt row until 13 sts rem.

Next row (RS) (buttonhole): MP, K2tog, K until 8 sts rem on **left needle,** cast off next 5 sts, K to end.

Next row (WS): K3, (yon) 5 times, K to end.

Next row: MP, K2tog, K to end, knitting into back of each of the 5 loops.

Work 1 row.

Next row: MP, K2tog, K to end.

Next row (WS): K to last 3 sts K2tog, K1.

Dec (at same edge) as before on every row until 6 sts rem, ending with a WS row.

Next row (RS): MP, K3tog, K to end.

Next row: K3tog, K1.
Cast off rem 2 sts, but do not break yarn.

Upper right front

With RS of work facing, starting at side edge and using 4 mm (US 6) needles, pick up and knit 45 (48: 51: 53: 56: 59) sts evenly along the top (straight) edge of peplum and work in patt as folls:

Row 1(WS): P to last 10 sts, K to end.
Rows 2, 4 and 6: MP, K to end.
Row 3: P1 (4: 1: 3: 6: 3), (cluster 3, P3) to last 14 sts, cluster 3, P1, K10.
Row 5: P to last 10 sts, K to end.
Row 7: P4 (1: 4: 6: 3: 6), (cluster 3, P3) to last 11 sts, P1, K10.
Row 8: MP, K to end.

These 8 rows form patt and are repeated throughout.
Cont in patt as set, remembering not to work any cluster less than 1 st away from side edges.
Work 1 row straight, ending with a WS row.
Next row (RS) (inc): MP, K to last 2 sts, M1, K2.
46 (49: 52: 54: 57: 60) sts.
Work 9 rows straight, ending with a WS row.
Next row (RS) (inc): MP, K to last 2 sts, M1, K2.
47 (50: 53: 55: 58: 61) sts.
Work 7 (7: 7: 9: 9: 9) rows straight, ending with a WS row.
Next row (RS): MP, K10, K2tog, K to last 2 sts, M1, K2.
Work 7 rows.
Rep last 8 rows 3 times more, ending with a WS row.
Next row (RS) (dec): MP, K10, K2tog, K to end.
46 (49: 52: 54: 57: 60) sts.
Work 2 (2: 6: 4: 6: 10) rows straight, ending with a **RS** row. (Right front should now match back to beg of armhole shaping.)

Shape armhole

Keeping patt correct, dec as before at neck edge on 8th row from previous dec, then on 6 (6: 6: 7: 7: 7) foll 8th rows, and **at the same time** shape armhole as folls:
Cast off 4 sts at beg of next row.
Dec 1 st at armhole edge of next 5 (5: 5: 5: 7: 7) rows, then on 1 (2: 3: 3: 3: 4) foll alt rows, then on foll 4th row.
28 (30: 32: 33: 34: 36) sts.
Work 4 (6: 10: 4: 6: 8) rows straight, ending with a **RS** row. (Right front should now match back to start of shoulder shaping.)

Shape shoulder

Cast off 6 (7: 7: 8: 8: 9) sts at beg of next row and foll alt row.
Work 1 row.
Cast off 6 (6: 8: 7: 8: 8) sts, patt to end.
Next row (WS): MP, knit to end, inc 1 st at end of row. 11 sts.
Keeping picot edging correct as set, cont in garter stitch for a further 24 rows.
Cast off.

SLEEVES (both alike)

Cuff (knitted from side to side)

Cast on 12 sts using 3 ¼ mm (US 3) needles and work in garter stitch as folls:
Knit 2 rows, ending with a WS row.
Next row (RS): MP, K to end.
Next row: Knit.
Working a picot at beg of every **RS** row, cont for a further 102 (106: 110: 114: 118: 122) rows, ending with a WS row.
Cast off, but do not break yarn.

Upper sleeve

With RS of cuff facing and using 4 mm (US 6) needles pick up and knit 53 (55: 57: 59: 61: 63) sts evenly along the top (straight) edge of cuff and purl 1 row, ending with a WS row.
Cont in patt as folls:
Rows 1, 3, 5 and 7: Knit.
Row 2: P1 (2: 3: 4: 5: 6), (cluster 3, P3) to last 4 (5: 6: 7: 8: 9) sts, cluster 3, P1 (2: 3: 4: 5: 6).
Rows 4: Purl.
Row 6: P4 (5: 6: 1: 2: 3), (cluster 3, P3) to last 1 (2: 3: 4: 5: 6) sts, (cluster 3) 0 (0: 0: 1: 1: 1) times, P1 (2: 3: 1: 2: 3).
Row 8: Purl.
These 8 rows form patt and are repeated throughout.
Keeping patt correct as set, cont as folls:
Work 1 (1: 1: 3: 3: 3) rows straight, ending with a WS row.
Next row (RS) (inc): K2, M1, K to last 2 sts, M1, K2.
55 (57: 59: 61: 63: 65) sts.
Working all incs as set by last row, cont in patt, inc 1 st at each end of every foll 10th (10th: 10th: 10th: 12th: 12th) row until there are 69 (71: 73: 75: 67: 69) sts.

XL & XXL sizes only

Inc at each end of every foll 10th row until there are 77 (79) sts.

All sizes

Work 5 (7: 11: 7: 11: 15) rows straight, ending with a WS row. (Sleeve should meas approx 36 (37.5: 39: 40: 41.5: 43) cm.)

Shape sleeve top

Cast off 4 sts at beg of next 2 rows.
61 (63: 65: 67: 69: 71) sts.
Dec 1 st at each end of next 3 rows, then on foll alt row, then on foll 4th row.
51 (53: 55: 57: 59: 61) sts.
Work 5 rows.
Dec 1 st at each end of next and every foll 6th row until 47 (47: 49: 49: 51: 53) sts rem, then on foll 4th row, then on every foll alt row until 37 (41: 43: 43: 47: 45) sts rem.
Dec 1 st at each end of every foll row until 27 (27: 29: 33: 33: 35) sts rem, ending with a WS row.
Cast off rem 27 (27: 29: 33: 33: 35) sts.

MAKING UP

Join shoulder seams using back stitch or mattress stitch if preferred.
With RS facing, join the cast-off edges of garter stitch bands neatly together and slip stitch in place around back neck.
Machine wash all pieces together before completing sewing up.
Join side and sleeve seams.
Set sleeve into armhole.
Sew on button.

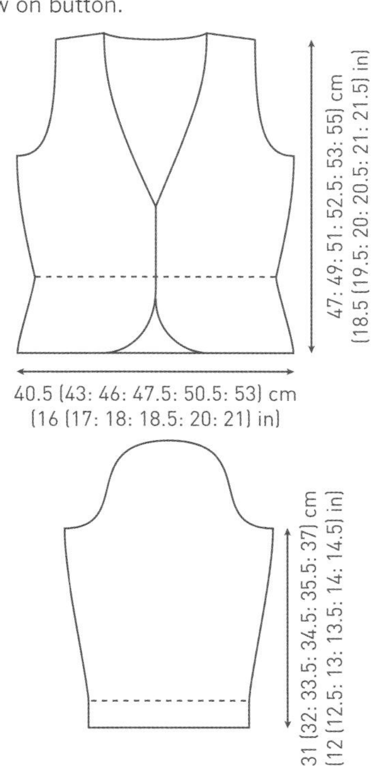

SUNLIT

SEMI FITTED TUNIC WITH CABLES & GARTER STITCH YOKE

Recommendation
Suitable for the knitter with a little experience
Please see pages 22 & 23 for photographs.

	XS	S	M	L	XL	XXL	
To fit	**81**	**86**	**91**	**97**	**102**	**107**	**cm**
bust	32	34	36	38	40	42	in

Rowan Purelife Organic Cotton
Photographed in Natural
9 10 11 11 12 12 x50gm

Needles
1 pair 3 ¼ mm (no 10) (US 3) needles
1 pair 3 ¾ mm (no 9) (US 5) needles
Cable needle
3 mm (no 11) (US 2/3) circular needle
3 ¼ mm (no 10) (US 3) circular needle

Tension
22 sts and 30 rows to 10 cm measured over textured stitch using 3 ¾ mm (US 5) needles

BACK AND FRONT (both alike)
Cast on 109 (115: 119: 125: 131: 139) sts using 3 ¼ mm (US 3) needles and work lower edging, setting stitches as folls:
Row 1 (RS): P0 (0: 1: 1: 1: 0), (K1b, P1) 8 (9: 9: 10: 11: 13) times, *K2, P1, K26, P1, K2 *, P1, (K1b, P1) 6 (7: 8: 9: 10: 11) times, rep from * to *, (P1, K1b) to last 0 (0: 1: 1: 1: 0) st, P0 (0: 1: 1: 1: 0).
Row 2 : K16 (18: 19: 21: 23: 26), *P2, K1, P4, K3, P4, K4, P4, K3, P4, K1, P2 *, K13 (15: 17: 19: 21: 23), rep from * to *, K16 (18: 19: 21: 23: 26).
These 2 rows set the stitches for the cable panels and the textured patt.
Rep the last 2 rows 4 times more, ending with a WS row.
Change to 3 ¾ mm (US 5) needles and work cable panels from chart and setting sts as folls:**Row 1 (RS):** Patt 16 (18: 19: 21: 23: 26), work 32 sts from **chart A** row 1, patt 13 (15: 17: 19: 21: 23), work 32 sts from **chart B** row 1, patt to end.
Row 2: K16 (18: 19: 21: 23: 26), work 32 sts from **chart B** row 2, K13 (15: 17: 19: 21: 23), work 32 sts from **chart A** row 2, K to end.
These 2 rows set the stitches.
Cont on sts as set, working the cable panels from chart, repeating the 20 row rep throughout and **at the same time** shape sides as folls:
Work 2 (2: 2: 4: 4: 4) rows.
Dec 1 st at each end of next row and 4 foll 6th rows, ending with a **RS** row.
99 (105: 109: 115: 121: 129) sts.
Work 21 rows.
Inc 1 st at each end of next row and 4 (6: 6: 6: 4: 2) foll 8th rows and then on 2 (0: 0: 0: 2: 4) foll 6th (-: -: -:10th: 10th) rows.
113 (119: 123: 129: 135: 143) sts.
Work 9 (9: 11: 13: 11: 11) rows straight (back should measure approx 38 (39: 40: 41: 42: 43) cm), ending with a WS row.
Shape raglans
Cast off 6 (6: 6: 7: 7: 8) sts at beg of next 2 rows. 101 (107: 111: 115: 121: 127) sts.

Next row (RS)(dec): P1, P2tog, patt to last 3 sts, P2tog tbl, P1.
99 (105: 109: 113: 119: 125) sts.
Work 1 row.
Dec 1 st as before at each end of next row and every foll alt row until 81 (85: 89: 89: 93: 97) sts rem, ending with a **RS** row.
Work 1 row.
Cast off, taking 2 sts together over cables.

Sleeves (both alike)
Cast on 103 (105: 107: 109: 113: 117) sts using 3 ¼ mm (US 3) needles and work lower edging, setting stitches as folls:
Row 1 (RS): P1 (0: 1: 1: 1: 1), (K1b, P1) 10 (11: 11: 11: 12: 13) times, *K2, P1, K18, P1, K2 *, P1, (K1b, P1) 6 (6: 6: 7: 7: 7) times, rep from * to *, (P1, K1b) to last 1 (0: 1: 1: 1: 1) st, P1 (0: 1: 1: 1: 1).
Row 2: K21 (22: 23: 23: 25: 27), *P2, K1, P4, (K3, P4) twice, K1, P2, K13 (13: 13: 15: 15: 15), rep from * to *, K21 (22: 23: 23: 25: 27).
These 2 rows set the stitches for the cable panels and the textured patt.
Rep the last 2 rows 3 times more, ending with a WS row.
Change to 3 ¾ mm (US 5) needles and work cable panels from chart and setting sts as folls:
Row 1 (RS): Patt 21 (22: 23: 23: 25: 27), work 24 sts from **chart C** row 1, patt 13 (13: 13: 15: 15: 15), work 24 sts from **chart D** row 1, patt to end.
Row 2: K21 (22: 23: 23: 25: 27), work 24 sts from **chart D** row 2, K13 (13: 13: 15: 15: 15), work 24 sts from **chart C** row 2, K to end.
These 2 rows set the stitches.
Cont on sts as set, working the cable panels from chart, repeating the 20 row rep throughout until sleeve measures approx 17 (18: 19: 20: 21: 22) cm, ending with the same pattern row as back and ending with a WS row.
Shape raglan
Cast off 6 (6: 6: 7: 7: 8) sts at beg of next 2 rows.
91 (93: 95: 95: 99: 101) sts.

XS, S & M sizes only:
Next row (RS)(dec): P1, P2tog, patt to last 3 sts, P2tog tbl, P1. 89 (91: 93) sts.
Next row (dec): K1, K2tog tbl, Patt to last 3 sts, K2tog, K1. 87 (89: 91) sts.
Rep the last 2 rows 2 (1: 1) times more and then first row again, ending with a **RS** row. 77 (83: 85) sts.
Work 1 row.
XXL size only:
Next row (RS)(dec): P1, P2tog, patt to last 3 sts, P2tog tbl, P1. 99 sts.
Work 3 rows, ending with a WS row.
All sizes:
Next row (RS)(dec): P1, P2tog, patt to last 3 sts, P2tog tbl, P1. 75 (81: 83: 93: 97: 97) sts.
Work 1 row.
Dec 1 st as before at each end of next row and every foll alt row until 65 (67: 69: 69: 71: 73) sts rem, ending with a **RS** row.
Work 1 row.
Cast off, taking 2 sts together over cables.

Making up
Pin out the pieces, cover with a dry cloth and steam.
Leave knitting to set before removing pins.
Join three raglan seams using back stitch or mattress st if preferred, leaving the left back seam open.
Neck edging
With RS of left sleeve top facing, and using a 3 ¼ mm (US 3) circular needle, pick up and knit 55 (57: 59: 59: 61: 63) sts across left sleeve top, 67 (71: 75: 75: 79: 83) sts across front neck, 55 (57: 59: 59: 61: 63) sts across right sleeve top and 67 (71: 75: 75: 79: 83) sts across back neck.
244 (256: 268: 268: 280: 292) sts.
Next row (WS)(dec): K66 (70: 74: 74: 78: 82), K2tog, place a marker around this last st, K53 (55: 57: 57: 59: 61), K2tog, place a marker around this last st and another halfway across sleeve top stitches (to denote shoulder line), K65 (69: 73: 73: 77: 81), K2tog (place a marker around this last st), K to end, placing a marker on 27th (28th: 29th: 29th: 30th: 31st) of these sts (to denote shoulder line).
241 (253: 265: 265: 277: 289) sts.
Cont in garter st, i.e. K every row, shaping edging as folls:
Work 4 rows, ending with a WS row.
Next row (RS)(dec): K2, K2tog tbl, * K to 3 sts before next marker, K2tog, K3, K2tog tbl; rep from * 4 times more, K to last 4 sts, K2tog, K2.
229 (241: 253: 253: 265: 277) sts.
Work 3 rows.
Rep the last 4 rows three times more, and then the dec row once more, ending with a **RS** row.
181 (193: 205: 205: 217: 229) sts.
Change to 3 mm (US 2/3) circular needle.
Work 5 rows, ending with a WS row.
Work the dec row once more, ending with a WS row.
169 (181: 193: 193: 205: 217) sts.
Cast off knitwise (on WS), casting off quite firmly over sleeve tops.
Join rem raglan seam.
Join side and sleeve seams.

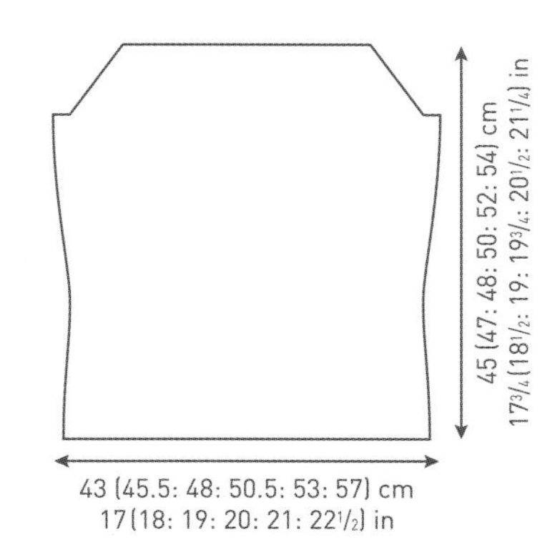

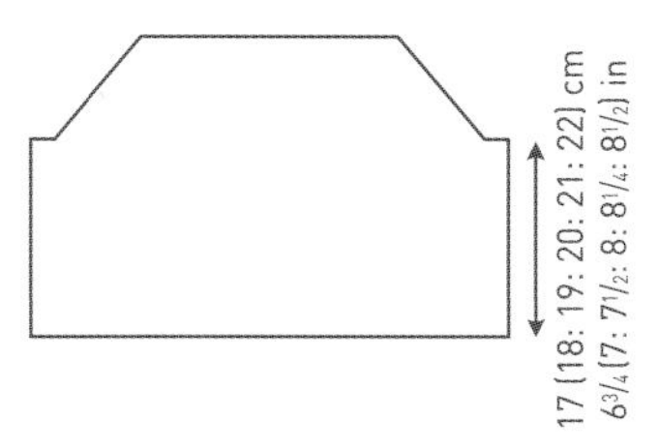

Please Note: These measurements do not include the neck edging.

Key
K on RS, P on WS
P on RS, K on WS
Slip 2 sts onto cn, hold at back, K2, K2 from cn.
Slip 2 sts onto cn, hold at front, K2, K2 from cn.
Slip 1 st onto cn, hold at back, K2, P1 from cn.
Slip 2 sts onto cn, hold at front, P1, K2 from cn.

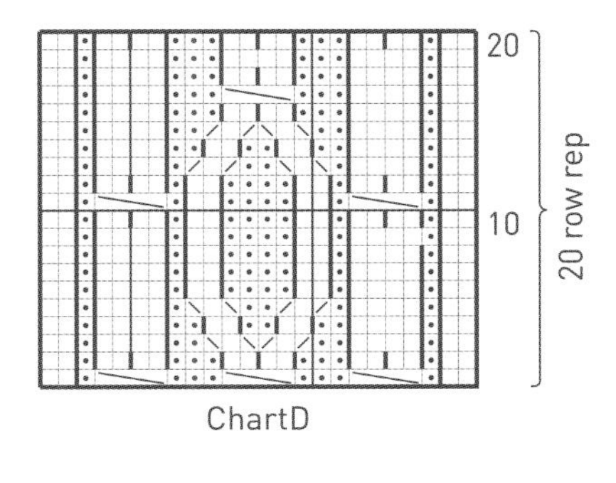

ChartD

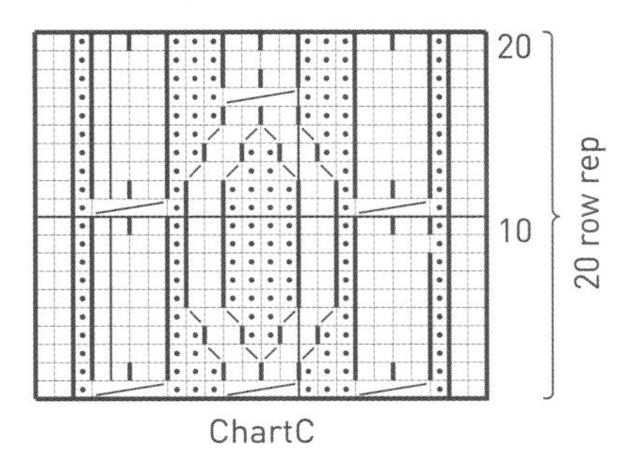

ChartC

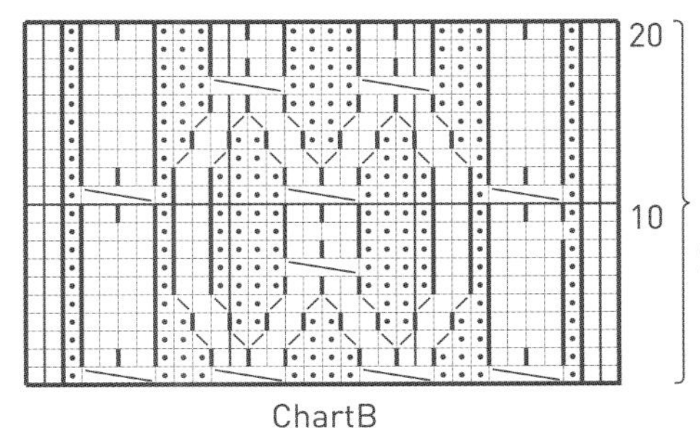

ChartB

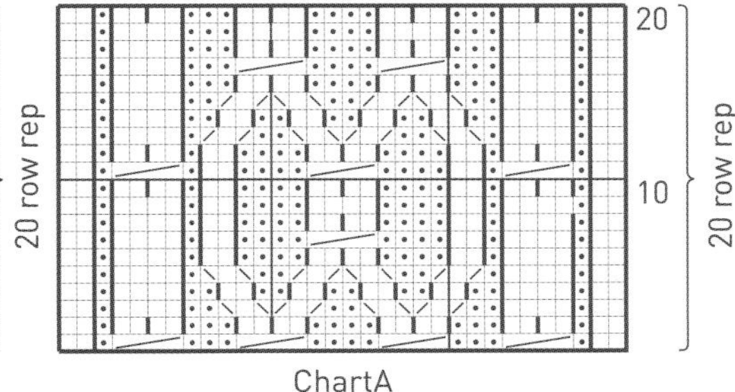

ChartA

ORCHID

PRETTY FITTED CARDIGAN WITH SHAPED PEPLUM

Recommendation
Suitable for the more experienced knitter.
Please see pages 28 – 31 for photographs.

	XS	S	M	L	XL	XXL	
To fit	**81**	**86**	**91**	**97**	**102**	**109**	**cm**
bust	32	34	36	38	40	43	in

Rowan Purelife Organic Cotton
Photographed in Yellowwood

9	10	11	11	12	12	x50gm

Buttons · 8

Needles
1 pair 3 mm (no 11) (US 2/3) needles
1 pair 3 ¾ mm (no 9) (US 5) needles

Tension
23 sts and 34 rows to 10cm measured over textured stitch using 3 ¾ mm (US 5) needles

Textured stitch
Row 1 (RS): K1, (P1, K1) to end.
Row 2: Knit.
These 2 rows form the pattern.

BACK
Cast on 149 (155: 161: 177: 183: 191) sts using 3 ¾ mm (US 5) needles, work flounce and shape lower edge, setting sts as folls:
Short row shaping rows 1 & 2: K0 (1: 0: 1: 0: 0), (P1, K1) 10 (11: 13: 13: 15: 17) times, (20 (23: 26: 27: 30: 34) sts now on right needle), P15 (15: 15: 17: 17: 17), K1, (P1, K1) 5 (5: 5: 6: 6: 6) times, P15 (15: 15: 17: 17: 17), K1, (P1, K1) 13 (13: 13: 14: 14: 14) times, wrap next st (by slipping next st onto right needle, taking yarn to opposite side of work between needles and then slipping same st back onto left needle) and turn, K27 (27: 27: 29: 29: 29), wrap next st and turn.
Short row shaping rows 3 & 4: K1, (P1, K1) 13 (13: 13: 14: 14: 14) times, P15 (15: 15: 17: 17: 17), K1, (P1, K1) 5 (5: 5: 6: 6: 6) times, wrap next st and turn, K79 (79: 79: 89: 89: 89), wrap next st and turn.
Short row shaping rows 5 & 6: K1, (P1, K1) 5 (5: 5: 6: 6: 6) times, P15 (15: 15: 17: 17: 17), K1, (P1, K1) 13 (13: 13: 14: 14: 14) times, P15 (15: 15: 17: 17: 17), K1, (P1, K1) 5 (5: 5: 6: 6: 6) times, P15 (15: 15: 17: 17: 17), (K1, P1) 4 (4: 4: 6: 6: 6) times, wrap next st and turn, K125 (125: 125: 147: 147: 147) sts, wrap next st and turn.
Short row shaping rows 7 & 8: (P1, K1) 4 (4: 4: 6: 6: 6) times, P15 (15: 15: 17: 17: 17), K1, (P1, K1) 5 (5: 5: 6: 6: 6) times, P15 (15: 15: 17: 17: 17), K1, (P1, K1) 13 (13: 13: 14: 14: 14) times, P15 (15: 15: 17: 17: 17), K1, (P1, K1) 5 (5: 5: 6: 6: 6) times, P15 (15: 15: 17: 17: 17), (K1, P1) 8 (8: 8: 11: 11: 11) times, wrap next st and turn, K to the last 4 (7: 10: 5: 8: 12) sts, wrap next st and turn.
Row 9 (RS): (P1, K1) 8 (8: 8: 11: 11: 11) times, P15 (15: 15: 17: 17: 17), K1, (P1, K1) 5 (5: 5: 6: 6: 6) times, P15 (15: 15: 17: 17: 17), K1, (P1, K1) 13 (13: 13: 14: 14: 14) times, P15 (15: 15: 17: 17: 17), K1, (P1, K1) 5 (5: 5: 6: 6: 6) times, P15 (15: 15: 17: 17: 17), (K1, P1) to last 0 (1: 0: 1: 0: 0) st, K0 (1: 0: 1: 0: 0).
Row 10: Knit.
The last 2 rows set the sts for the flounce.
Place a marker on the needle at each side of the four **rev st st** panels · 8 markers in total.
Slip the markers from left to right needle on next and every foll row up to top of flounce.
Keeping sts correct cont as folls:
Work 2 rows.
Row 1 (RS)(dec): Patt 2tog, *patt to next marker, P2tog, P to 2 sts before next marker, P2tog tbl; rep from * 3 times more, patt to last 2 sts, patt 2tog.
139 (145: 151: 167: 173: 181) sts.
Work 3 rows.
Dec 1 st at each end of next row and foll 4th row.
135 (141: 147: 163: 169: 177) sts.
Cont to dec 1 st at each end of every 4th row until 10 (10: 10: 11: 11: 11) side decs in all completed, and **at the same time** shape **rev st st** panels as folls:
Keeping side shaping correct work 1 row.
Row 11 (RS)(dec): *patt to next marker, P2tog, P to 2 sts before next marker, P2tog tbl; rep from * 3 times more, patt to end.
Work 7 rows.
Row 19: Work as row 11.
Work 5 rows.
Row 25 (RS)(dec): Work as row 1.
Work 3 rows.
Rep the last 4 rows 2 (2: 2: 3: 3: 3) times more, ending with a WS row.
Next row (RS)(dec): Patt 2tog, *patt to next marker, P3tog, ignore marker directly after these 3 sts; rep from * 3 times more, patt to last 2 sts, patt 2tog.
73 (79: 85: 91: 97: 105) sts.
Work 1 row.

Place a marker at each end of this row.
Keeping patt correct cont shaping sides as folls:
Work 8 rows, ending with a WS row.
Inc 1 st at each end of next row and 3 (3: 5: 5: 5: 5) foll 8th rows and then on every foll 6th row to 93 (99: 105: 111: 117: 125) sts.
Work straight until back measures 23 (23: 24: 24: 24: 24) cm from markers.

Shape armholes
Cast off 4 (4: 4: 4: 5: 6) sts at beg of next 2 rows.
85 (91: 97: 103: 107: 113) sts.
Dec 1 st at each end of next 3 rows, then on 3 (4: 5: 6: 6: 7) foll alt rows, and then on foll 4th row.
71 (75: 79: 83: 87: 91) sts.
Work straight until armhole measures 18 (19: 19: 20: 21: 22) cm, ending with a WS row.

Shape shoulders and back neck
Cast off 6 (6: 6: 7: 7: 7) sts at beg of next 2 rows.
Cast off 5 (6: 6: 6: 6: 7) sts, patt until there are 9 (9: 10: 10: 11: 11) sts on right needle and turn, leaving rem sts on a holder.
Work each side of neck separately.
Cast off 4 sts, work to end.
Cast off rem 5 (5: 6: 6: 7: 7) sts.
With RS facing rejoin yarn to rem sts, cast off centre 31 (33: 35: 37: 39: 41) sts, patt to end.
Complete to match first side, reversing shapings.

Left front
Cast on 80 (83: 86: 93: 96: 100) sts using 3 ¾ mm (US 5) needles and work flounce and shape lower edge, setting sts as folls:
Short row shaping rows 1 & 2: K0 (1: 0: 1: 0: 0), (P1, K1) 2 (3: 5: 2: 4: 6) times, wrap next st and turn, K to end.
Short row shaping rows 3 & 4: K0 (1: 0: 1: 0: 0), (P1, K1) 6 (7: 9: 7: 9: 11) times, wrap next st and turn, K to end.
These rows set the sts for the textured stitch.
Short row shaping rows 5 & 6 (dec): Patt 2 tog, keeping patt correct, working in rib patt until 19 (22: 25: 26: 29: 33) sts on right needle, wrap next st and turn, K to end.
79 (82: 85: 92: 95: 99) sts.
Row 7 (RS): Patt 19 (22: 25: 26: 29: 33), P13 (13: 13: 15: 15: 15), K1 (P1, K1) 5 (5: 5: 6: 6: 6) times, P13 (13: 13: 15: 15: 15), K1, (P1, K1) to end.
Row 8: (K1, P1) twice, K to end.
The last 2 rows set the sts for the flounce and the 5 sts at front edge which are worked in **moss st** up the entire front edge.
Place a marker on the needle at each side of the two **rev st st** panels - 4 markers in total.
Slip the markers from left to right needle on next and every foll row up to top of flounce.
Keeping front edge and flounce sts correct cont as folls:
Dec 1 st at beg of next row. 78 (81: 84: 91: 94: 98) sts.
Work 3 rows.
Dec 1 st at beg of next row and every foll 4th row until 10 (10: 10: 11: 11: 11) side dec in all completed.
Work 1 row.
Row 1 (RS)(dec): *patt to next marker, P2tog, P to 2 sts before next marker, P2tog tbl; rep from * once more, patt to end.
74 (77: 80: 87: 90: 94) sts.
Keeping side shaping correct, work 7 rows.
Row 9: Work as row 1.
Work 5 rows.
Row 15 (RS)(dec): Patt 2tog, *patt to next marker, P2tog, P to 2 sts before next marker, P2tog tbl; rep from * once more, patt to end.
Work 3 rows.
Rep the last 4 rows 2 (2: 2: 3: 3: 3) times more, ending with a WS row.
Next row (RS)(dec): Patt 2tog, *patt to next marker, P3tog, ignore marker directly after these 3 sts; rep from * once more, patt to end.
46 (49: 52: 54: 57: 61) sts.
Work 1 row.
Place a marker at each end of this row.
Keeping front edge sts and patt correct cont shaping side as folls:
Work 8 rows, ending with a WS row.
Inc 1 st at beg of next row and 3 (3: 5: 5: 5: 5) foll 8th rows and then on every foll 6th row to 56 (59: 62: 64: 67: 71) sts.
Work straight until front matches back to beg of armhole shaping, ending with a WS row.

Shape armhole
Cast off 4 (4: 4: 4: 5: 6) sts at beg of next row.
52 (55: 58: 60: 62: 65) sts.
Work 1 row.
Dec 1 st at armhole edge on next 3 rows, then on 3 (4: 5: 6: 6: 7) foll alt rows, and then on foll 4th row. 45 (47: 49: 50: 52: 54) sts.
Work straight until front is 24 (24: 26: 26: 28: 28) rows shorter than back to shoulder shaping, ending with a WS row.

Shape front neck
Next row (RS): Patt 28 (29: 29: 30: 33: 34) and turn, leaving rem 17 (18: 20: 20: 19: 20) sts on a holder for neck edging.
Dec 1 st at neck edge on next 6 (6: 4: 4: 6: 6) rows, then on 5 foll alt rows, and then 1 (1: 2: 2: 2: 2) foll 4th rows. 16 (17: 18: 19: 20: 21) sts.
Work 3 rows, ending with a WS row.

Shape shoulder
Cast off 6 (6: 6: 7: 7: 7) sts at beg of next row and 5 (6: 6: 6: 6: 7) sts at beg of foll alt row.
Work 1 row.
Cast off rem 5 (5: 6: 6: 7: 7) sts.

Mark position of 8 buttons, the first to come on row after marked row at waistline, the 8th will come 2 rows above neck edge (to be made in neck edging) and rem 6 spaced evenly between.

Right front
Cast on 80 (83: 86: 93: 96: 100) sts using 3 ¾ mm (US 5) needles and work flounce and shape lower edge, setting sts as folls:
Row 1 (RS): K1, (P1, K1) 11 times, P13 (13: 13: 15: 15: 15), K1, (P1, K1) 5 (5: 5: 6: 6: 6) times, P13 (13: 13: 15: 15: 15), (K1, P1) to last 0 (1: 0: 1: 0: 0) st, K0 (1: 0: 1: 0: 0).
Short row shaping rows 2 & 3: K4 (7: 10: 5: 8: 12), wrap next st and turn, work in rib patt to end.
Short row shaping rows 4 & 5: K12 (15: 18: 15: 18: 22), wrap next st and turn, patt to last 2 sts, patt 2tog.
79 (82: 85: 92: 95: 99) sts.
Short row shaping rows 6 & 7: K20 (23: 26: 27: 30: 34), wrap next st and turn, patt to end.
Row 8: K to last 4 sts, (P1, K1) twice.
The last 2 rows set the sts for the flounce.
Place a marker on the needle at each side of the two **rev st st** panels - 4 markers in total.
Slip the markers from left to right needle on next and every foll row up to top of flounce.
Keeping front edge and flounce sts correct cont as folls:
Dec 1 st at end of next row.
78 (81: 84: 91: 94: 98) sts.
Work 3 rows.
Dec 1 st at end of next row and every foll 4th row until 10 (10: 10: 11: 11: 11) side dec in all completed.
Work 1 row.

Row 1 (RS)(dec): *patt to next marker, P2tog, P to 2 sts before next marker, P2tog tbl; rep from * once more, patt to end.
74 (77: 80: 87: 90: 94) sts.
Keeping side shaping correct, work 7 rows.
Row 9: Work as row 1.
Work 5 rows.
Row 15 (RS)(dec): *patt to next marker, P2tog, P to 2 sts before next marker, P2tog tbl; rep from * once more, patt to last 2 sts, patt 2tog.
Work 3 rows.
Rep the last 4 rows 2 (2: 2: 3: 3: 3) times more, ending with a WS row.
Next row (RS)(dec): *patt to next marker, P3tog, ignore marker directly after these 3 sts; rep from * once more, patt to last 2 sts, patt 2tog.
46 (49: 52: 54: 57: 61) sts.
Work 1 row.
Place a marker at each end of this row.
Next row (RS)(buttonhole): Patt 4 sts, yon, patt 2tog, patt to end.
Work 1 row.
Keeping front edge sts and patt correct cont shaping side as folls:
Work 8 rows, ending with a WS row.
Complete to match left front, reversing shapings and working buttonholes as before to correspond with positions marked for buttons.

Sleeves
Right sleeve
Sleeve front:
Cast on 36 (37: 38: 39: 41: 42) sts using 3 mm (US 2/3) needles and work as folls:
*Knit 3 rows, ending with a **RS** row.
Next row (WS): K0 (1: 0: 1: 1: 0), (P1, K1) to end.
Next row: (K1, P1) to last 0 (1: 0: 1: 1: 0) st, K0 (1: 0: 1: 1: 0).
Rep these 2 rows twice more, ending with a **RS** row.**
Break yarn and leave sts on a spare needle.
Sleeve back:
Cast on 28 (29: 30: 31: 33: 34) sts using 3 mm (US 2/3) needles and work as for sleeve front from * to **.
Join edgings together:
Next row (WS): Knit to last 7 sts, now holding **sleeve back** in front of **sleeve front** (as they face you), and taking 1 st from each needle together at the same time, K7, K to end.
57 (59: 61: 63: 67: 69) sts.
Change to 3 ¾ mm (US 5) needles and cont in patt setting the sts as folls:
Row 1 (RS): P1, (K1, P1) to end.
Row 2: Knit.
These 2 rows form the patt.
Keeping patt correct throughout, cont shaping sides as folls:
Work 6 rows.
Inc 1 st at each end of next row.
59 (61: 63: 65: 69: 71) sts.
Work 17 rows, ending with a WS row.
Inc 1 st at each end of next row and every foll 16th (16th: 16th: 16th: 18th: 18th) to 69 (71: 73: 75: 79: 81) sts, ending with a **RS** row.
Work straight until sleeve measures 32 (33: 34: 35: 36: 37) cm, ending with a WS row.
Shape sleeve top
Cast off 4 (4: 4: 4: 5: 6) sts at beg of next 2 rows.
61 (63: 65: 67: 69: 69) sts.
Dec 1 st at each end of next 3 rows, then on foll alt row, and then on every foll 4th row to 41 (41: 43: 43: 45: 43) sts, ending with a **RS** row.
Work 1 row.
Dec 1 st at each end of next row and 2 (2: 2: 2: 3: 4) foll alt rows and then on every foll row until 25 (25: 27: 27: 27: 27) sts rem.
Cast off 3 sts at beg of next 2 rows.
Cast off rem 19 (19: 21: 21: 21: 21) sts.

Left sleeve
Sleeve back:
Cast on 28 (29: 30: 31: 33: 34) sts using 3 mm (US 2/3) needles and work as folls:
*Knit 3 rows, ending with a **RS** row.
Next row (WS): K0 (1: 0: 1: 1: 0), (P1, K1) to end.
Next row: (K1, P1) to last 0 (1: 0: 1: 1: 0) st, K0 (1: 0: 1: 1: 0).
Rep these 2 rows twice more, ending with a **RS** row.**
Break yarn and leave sts on a spare needle.
Sleeve front:
Cast on 36 (37: 38: 39: 41: 42) sts using 3 mm (US 2/3) needles and work as for sleeve back from * to **.
Join edgings together:
Next row (WS): Knit to last 7 sts, now holding **sleeve front** in front of sleeve back (as they face you), and taking 1 st from each needle together at the same time, K7, K to end.
57 (59: 61: 63: 67: 69) sts.
Change to 3 ¾ mm (US 5) needles and complete as given for right sleeve.

Making up
Join shoulder seams, using back stitch or mattress st if preferred.
Neck edging
With RS of right front facing and using 3 mm (US 2/3) needles, slip 17 (18: 20: 20: 19: 20) sts from holder onto right needle, rejoin yarn and pick up and knit 24 (24: 26: 26: 28: 28) sts up right front neck, 39 (41: 43: 45: 47: 49) sts across back and 24 (24: 26: 26: 28: 28) sts down left front, work in patt across 17 (18: 20: 20: 19: 20) sts on holder. 121 (125: 135: 137: 141: 145) sts.
Cont in moss st as folls:
Keeping moss st patt correct:
Work 1 row.
Next row (RS)(buttonhole): Work 4 sts, yon, patt 2tog, patt to end.
Work 4 rows, ending with a **RS** row.
Cast off in patt.
Join side and sleeve seams.
Set sleeves into armholes.
Sew on buttons to correspond with buttonholes.

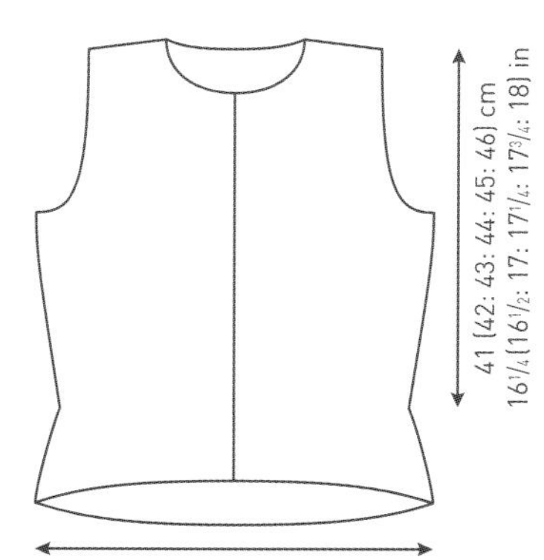

40.5 (43: 45.5: 48: 50.5: 54.5) cm
16 (17: 18: 19: 20: 21½) in

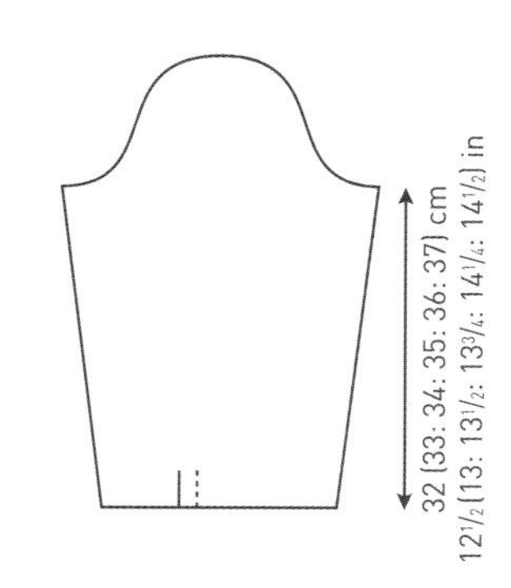

JOY

CLASSIC CARDIGAN WITH EYELET DETAIL

Recommendation
Suitable for the knitter with a little experience
Please see page 33 for photograph.

	XS	S	M	L	XL	XXL	
To fit	**81**	**86**	**91**	**97**	**102**	**107**	**cm**
bust	32	34	36	38	40	42	ins

Rowan Denim
Photographed in Ecru

10	11	11	12	12	13	x50gm

Needles
1 pair 3¼ mm (no 10) (US 3) needles
1 pair 4 mm (no 8) (US 6) needles

Buttons - 5

Tension
Before washing: 20 sts and 28 rows to 10 cm measured over stocking stitch using 4 mm (US 6) needles.

Tension note:
Denim will shrink in length when washed for the first time. Allowances have been made in the pattern for shrinkage (see size diagram for after washing measurements).

Special abbreviations:
Right dec = Sl 1, K1, psso, slip st now on right needle back onto left needle, lift 2nd st on left needle over this st and off left needle – 2 sts decreased.
Left dec = Sl 1, K2tog, psso – 2 sts decreased.

Eyelet ridge pattern
Row 1 (RS): Knit.
Row 2: Purl.
Rows 3 and 4: Knit.
Row 5: Purl.
Row 6: Knit.
Rows 7 to 12: As rows 1 to 6.
Rows 13 and 14: As rows 1 and 2.
Row 15: *K2tog, yfwd, rep from * to last st, K1.
Row 16: Purl.
Row 17: K1, *K2tog, yfwd, rep from * to last 2 sts, K2.
Row 18: Purl.
Rows 19 and 20: Knit.
Row 21: Purl.
Row 22: Knit.
Rows 23 to 32: As rows 13 to 22.
Rows 33 to 44: As rows 1 to 12.
Row 45: Purl.
Row 46: Knit.
Rows 47 and 48: As rows 45 and 46.

BACK
Cast on 159 (171: 177: 189: 201: 213) sts using 3¼ mm (US 3) needles and work edging as folls:
Row 1 (RS) (dec): K3, *cast off next 3 sts, K until there are 3 sts on right needle after cast-off, rep from * to end.
81 (87: 90: 96: 102: 108) sts.
Knit 7 rows, – (– : inc: inc: dec: dec) – (– : 1: 1: 1: 1) st at end of last row.
81 (87: 91: 97: 101: 107) sts.
Change to 4 mm (US 6) needles and cont in eyelet ridge patt as given above as folls:
Work 6 (6: 6: 8: 8: 8) rows straight, ending with a WS row.
Next row (RS) (dec): K2tog, K15 (17: 18: 20: 21: 23), left dec, K41 (43: 45: 47: 49: 51), right dec, K15 (17: 18: 20: 21: 23), K2tog.
75 (81: 85: 91: 95: 101) sts.
Work 21 (21: 21: 23: 23: 23) rows straight, ending with a WS row.
Next row (RS) (dec): K2tog, K13 (15: 16: 18: 19: 21), left dec, K39 (41: 43 : 45: 47: 49), right dec, K13 (15: 16: 18: 19: 21), K2tog.
69 (75: 79: 85: 89: 95) sts.
Work 27 rows straight, ending with a WS row.
Next row (RS) (inc): K2, M1, K12 (14: 15: 17: 18: 20), M1, K1, M1, K39 (41: 43 : 45: 47: 49), M1, K1, M1, K12 (14: 15: 17: 18: 20), M1, K2. 75 (81: 85: 91: 95: 101) sts.
Work 25 (25: 25: 27: 27: 27) rows straight, ending with a WS row.
Next row (RS) (inc): K2, M1, K14 (16: 17: 19: 20: 22), M1, K1, M1, K41 (43: 45: 47: 49: 51), M1, K1, M1, K14 (16: 17: 19: 20: 22) sts, M1, K2.
81 (87: 91: 97: 101: 107) sts.
Work 17 (19: 23: 19: 21: 25) rows straight, ending with a WS row. (Work should meas approx 37.5 (38: 39.5: 40: 40.5: 42) cm.)
Shape armholes
Keeping patt correct, cast off 3 (4: 4: 5: 5: 6) sts at beg of next 2 rows.
75 (79: 83: 87: 91: 95) sts.
Dec 1 st at each end of next 5 rows, then on 2 (3: 3: 3: 4: 4) foll alt rows, then on every foll 4th row until 59 (61: 65: 69: 71: 75) sts rem.
Cont straight until armhole meas 21 (22.5: 22.5: 23.5: 23.5: 24.5) cm, ending with a WS row.
Shape shoulders and back neck
Cast off 4 (4: 5: 5: 5: 6) sts at beg of next 2 rows.
51 (53: 55: 59: 61: 63) sts.
Next row (RS): Cast off 4 (4: 5: 5: 5: 6) sts, patt until there are 8 (8: 8: 9: 10: 9) sts on right needle and turn, leaving rem sts on a holder.
Work each side of neck separately.
Cast off 4 sts at beg of next row.
Cast off rem 4 (4: 4: 5: 6: 5) sts.
With RS facing, rejoin yarn to rem sts, cast off centre 27 (29: 29: 31: 31: 33) sts, patt to end.
Complete to match first side, reversing shapings.

LEFT FRONT
Cast on 87 (90: 90: 96: 102: 111) sts using 3¼ mm (US 3) needles and work edging as folls:
Row 1 (RS) (dec): K3, *cast off next 3 sts, K until there are 3 sts on right needle after cast-off, rep from * to last 3 sts, K3.
45 (48: 48: 51: 54: 57) sts.

Knit 7 rows dec (dec: inc: inc: – : –) 1 (1: 1: 1: – : –) st at end of last row.
44 (47: 49: 52: 54: 57) sts.
Change to 4 mm (US 6) needles and cont in eyelet ridge patt, keeping 6 sts at centre front in garter stitch throughout, as folls:
Work 6 (6: 6: 8: 8: 8) rows straight, ending with a WS row.
Next row (RS) (dec): K2tog, K15 (17: 18: 20: 21: 23), left dec, K to end.
41 (44: 46: 49: 51: 54) sts.
Work 21 (21: 21: 23: 23: 23) rows straight, ending with a WS row.
Next row (RS) (dec): K2tog, K13 (15: 16: 18: 19: 21), left dec, K to end.
38 (41: 43: 46: 48: 51) sts.
Work 27 rows straight, ending with a WS row.
Next row (RS) (inc): K2, M1, K12 (14: 15: 17: 18: 20), M1, K1, M1, K to end.
41 (44: 46: 49: 51: 54) sts.
Work 25 (25: 25: 27: 27: 27) rows straight, ending with a WS row.
Next row (RS) (inc): K2, M1, K14 (16: 17: 19: 20: 22), M1, K1, M1, K to end.
44 (47: 49: 52: 54: 57) sts.
Cont straight until left front matches back to beg of armhole shaping, ending with a WS row.

Shape armhole

Cast off 3 (4: 4: 5: 5: 6) sts at beg of next row.
41 (43: 45: 47: 49: 52) sts.
Work 1 row.
Dec 1 st at armhole edge of next 5 rows, then on 2 (3: 3: 3: 4: 4) foll alt rows, then on every foll 4th row until 33 (34: 36: 38: 39: 41) sts rem.
Cont straight until 15 (15: 17: 19: 19: 21) rows less have been worked than on back to start of shoulder shaping, ending with a **RS** row.

Shape neck

Patt 15 sts and leave these 15 sts on a holder for neck edging, patt to end.
Dec 1 st at neck edge on next 4 rows, then on 1 (2: 2: 3: 3: 4) foll alt rows, then on every foll 4th row until 12 (12: 14: 15: 16: 17) sts rem.
Work 4 (2:4: 4: 4: 4) rows straight, ending with a WS row.

Shape shoulder

Cast off 4 (4: 5: 5: 5: 6) sts at beg of next row and foll alt row.
Work 1 row. Cast off rem 4 (4: 4: 5: 6: 5) sts.
Mark position of 6 buttons, the fi rst to come in 6th row above fi rst dec row, the last one 8 rows down from beg of neck shaping and rem buttons spaced evenly between.

RIGHT FRONT

Cast on 87 (90: 90: 96: 102: 111) sts using 3¼ mm (US 3) needles and work edging as folls:
Row 1 (RS) (dec): K6, *cast off next 3 sts, K until there are 3 sts on right needle after cast-off, rep from * to end.
45 (48: 48: 51: 54: 57) sts.
Knit 7 rows dec (dec: inc: inc: – : –) 1 (1: 1: 1: – : –) st at beg of last row.
44 (47: 49: 52: 54: 57) sts.
Change to 4 mm (US 6) needles and cont in eyelet ridge patt, keeping 6 sts at centre front in garter stitch throughout, as folls:
Work 6 (6: 6: 8: 8: 8) rows straight, ending with a WS row.
Next row (RS) (dec): K24 (25: 26: 27: 28: 29), right dec, K15 (17: 18: 20: 21: 23), K2tog.
41 (44: 46: 49: 51: 54) sts.
Work 5 rows straight, ending with a WS row.
Next row (RS) (buttonhole row): K2, cast off 3, patt to end.
Next row: Work to position of cast-off sts on previous row, yon 3 times, K2.
Next row: K2, K into back of each loop, patt to end.
Working a further 5 buttonholes to correspond with positions marked for buttons on left front, cont as folls:
Work 13 (13: 13: 15: 15: 15) rows straight, ending with a WS row.
Next row (RS) (dec): K23 (24: 25: 26: 27: 28), right dec, K13 (15: 16: 18: 19: 21), K2tog.
38 (41: 43: 46: 48: 51) sts.
Work 27 rows straight, ending with a WS row.
Next row (RS) (inc): K23 (24: 25: 26: 27: 28), M1, K1, M1, K to last 2 sts, M1, K2.
41 (44: 46: 49: 51: 54) sts.
Work 25 (25: 25: 27: 27: 27) rows straight, ending with a WS row.
Next row (RS) (inc): K24 (25: 26: 27: 28: 29), M1, K1, M1, K to last 2 sts, M1, K2.
44 (47: 49: 52: 54: 57) sts.
Cont straight until right front matches back to beg of armhole shaping, ending with a **RS** row.

Shape armhole

Cast off 3 (4: 4: 5: 5: 6) sts at beg of next row.
41 (43: 45: 47: 49: 52) sts.
Dec 1 st at armhole edge of next 5 rows, then on 2 (3: 3: 3: 4: 4) foll alt rows, then on every foll 4th row until 33 (34: 36: 38: 39: 41) sts rem.
Cont straight until 14 (14: 16: 18: 18: 20) rows less have been worked than on back to start of shoulder shaping, ending with a WS row.

Shape neck

Patt 15 sts and leave these 15 sts on a holder for neck edging, patt to end.
Dec 1 st at neck edge on next 4 rows, then on 1 (2: 2: 3: 3: 4) foll alt rows, then on every foll 4th row until 12 (12: 14: 15: 16: 17) sts rem.
Work 4 (2:4: 4: 4: 4) rows straight, ending with a **RS** row.

Shape shoulder

Cast off 4 (4: 5: 5: 5: 6) sts at beg of next row and foll alt row.
Work 1 row.
Cast off rem 4 (4: 4: 5: 6: 5) sts.

SLEEVES (both alike)

Cast on 93 (93: 99: 105: 105: 111) sts using 3¼ mm (US 3) needles and work edging as folls:
Row 1 (RS) (dec): K3, *cast off next 3 sts, K until there are 3 sts on right needle after castoff, rep from * to end.
48 (48: 51: 54: 54: 57) sts.
Knit 7 (7: 9: 7: 9: 9) rows dec (inc: – : dec: inc: –) 1 (1: – : 1: 1: –) st at end of last row.
47 (49: 51: 53: 55: 57) sts.
Change to 4 mm (US 6) needles and cont in eyelet ridge patt, starting with patt row 9 (9: 13: 11: 13: 13), as folls:
Inc 1 st at each end of 7th (7th: 5th: 7th: 5th: 5th) row and every foll 14th row to 53 (55: 59: 63: 67: 69) sts, then on every foll 12th row until there are 61 (63: 65: 67: 69: 71) sts.
Work 11 rows straight, ending with a WS row.
(Sleeve should meas approx 35 (35: 35.5: 36.5: 37: 37) cm.)

Shape sleeve top

Keeping patt correct, cast off 3 (4: 4: 5: 5: 6) sts at beg of next 2 rows.
55 (55: 57: 57: 59: 59) sts.
Dec 1 st at each end of next 3 rows, then on foll alt row, then on foll 4th row.
45 (45: 47: 47: 49: 49) sts.
Work 5 rows.
Dec 1 st at each end of next and every foll 6th row until 37 (37: 39: 39: 41: 41) sts rem, then on foll 4th row, then on every foll alt row until 33 (31: 33: 31: 33: 31) sts rem.
Dec 1 st at each end of every foll row until 27 (25: 27: 21: 23: 21) sts rem, ending with a WS row.
Cast off rem 27 (25: 27: 21: 23: 21) sts.

MAKING UP

Join both shoulder seams using back stitch or mattress stitch if preferred.

Neck edge

With RS of right front facing and using 3¼ mm (US 3) needles, slip 15 sts from holder on right front onto the right needle, rejoin yarn and pick up and knit 16 (16: 18: 20: 20: 22) sts up right front neck, 35 (37: 37: 39: 39: 41) sts across back, and 16 (16: 18: 20: 20: 22) down left front neck, K across 15 sts from left front holder. 97 (99: 103: 109: 109: 115) sts.

Knit 6 rows, ending with a **RS** row.

Cast off knitwise on WS.

Machine wash all pieces together before completing sewing together.

Join side and sleeve seams.

Set sleeve into armhole.

Sew on buttons.

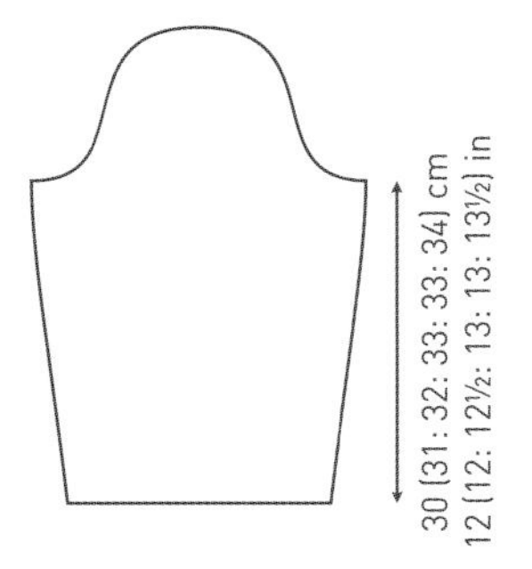

DAPPLE

TUNIC WITH CABLE PANELS & GENEROUS NECKLINE

Recommendation
Suitable for the more experienced knitter
Please see pages 34 – 37 for photographs.

	XS	S	M	L	XL	XXL	
To fit	**81**	**86**	**91**	**97**	**102**	**107**	**cm**
bust	32	34	36	38	40	42	in

Rowan All Seasons Cotton
Photographed in Smoke

12	12	13	14	14	15	x50gm

Needles
1 pair 4 ½ mm (no 7) (US 7) needles
1 pair 5 mm (no 6) (US 8) needles
Cable needle
4 mm (no 8) (US 6) circular needle
4 ½ mm (no 7) (US 7) circular needle

Tension
18 sts and 27 rows to 10 cm measured over reversed stocking stitch using 5 mm (US 8) needles

BACK AND FRONT (both alike)
Cast on 94 (98: 102: 106: 110: 118) sts, using 4 ½ mm (US 7) needles and work lower edging, setting stitches as folls:
Row 1 (RS): K2 (2: 0: 2: 0: 2), (P2, K2) to last 0 (0: 2: 0: 2: 0) sts, P0 (0: 2: 0: 2: 0).
Row 2: P2 (2: 0: 2: 0: 2), (K2, P2) to last 0 (0: 2: 0: 2: 0) sts, K0 (0: 2: 0: 2: 0).
These 2 rows set the stitches for the rib.
Cont in rib until 17 rows in all completed, ending with a **RS** row.
Next row (WS)(inc): Rib 26 (26: 28: 30: 32: 34), inc in each of next 2 sts, rib 38 (42: 42: 42: 42: 46), inc in each of next 2 sts, rib to end.
98 (102: 106: 110: 114: 122) sts.
Change to 5 mm (US 8) needles and set sts for cable panels as folls:
Row 1 (RS): P18 (18: 20: 22: 24: 26), work 20 sts from **chart A** row 1, P22 (26: 26: 26: 26: 30), work 20 sts from **chart B** row 1, P18 (18: 20: 22: 24: 26).
Row 2: K18 (18: 20: 22: 24: 26), work 20 sts from **chart B** row 2, K22 (26: 26: 26: 26: 30), work 20 sts from **chart A** row 2, K18 (18: 20: 22: 24: 26).
Cont on sts as set, working in patt from chart and rep the 24 row patt throughout, and **at the same time** shape sides as folls:
Work until chart row 20 completed, ending with a WS row.
Keeping patt correct, dec 1 st at each end of next row and 3 foll 8th rows and 3 foll 6th rows, ending with a **RS** row.
84 (88: 92: 96: 100: 108) sts.
Work 21 (21: 21: 23: 23: 23) rows.
Inc 1 st at each end of next row and 4 foll 10th rows, ending with a WS row.
94 (98: 102: 106: 110: 118) sts.
Work 9 (9: 11: 11: 11: 11) rows, ending with a WS row.
Shape raglans
Cast off 5 sts at beg of next 2 rows.
84 (88: 92: 96: 100: 108) sts.
XS size only:
Work 2 rows.
M, L, XL &XXL sizes only:
Dec 1 st at each end of next - (-: 3: 3: 3: 5) rows. - (-: 86: 90: 94: 98) sts.
Work 1 row.
All sizes:
Dec 1 st at each end of next row and every foll alt row until 68 (70: 72: 74: 76: 78) sts rem, ending with a **RS** row.
Work 1 row.
Cast off, taking 2 sts together over cables.

Left sleeve
Cast on 78 (80: 82: 84: 86: 88) sts using 4 ½ mm (US 7) needles and work lower edging setting sts as folls:
Row 1 (RS): K0 (0: 0: 1: 0: 0), P0 (1: 2: 2: 0: 1), (K2, P2) to last 2 (3: 0: 1: 2: 3) sts, K2 (2: 0: 1: 2: 2), P0 (1: 0: 0: 0: 1).
Row 2: P0 (0: 0: 1: 0: 0), K0 (1: 2: 2: 0: 1), (P2, K2) to last 2 (3: 0: 1: 2: 3) sts, P2 (2: 0: 1: 2: 2), K0 (1: 0: 0: 0: 1).
These 2 rows set the sts for the rib.
Cont in rib until 17 rows in all completed, ending with a **RS** row.
Next row (WS)(inc): Rib 38 (39: 40: 41: 42: 43), inc in each of next 2 sts, rib to end.
80 (82: 84: 86: 88: 90) sts.
Change to 5 mm (US 8) needles and set sts for cable panel as folls:***
Row 1 (RS): P30 (31: 32: 33: 34: 35), work 20 sts from **chart A** row 1, P30 (31: 32: 33: 34: 35).
Row 2: K30 (31: 32: 33: 34: 35), work 20 sts from **chart A** row 2, K30 (31: 32: 33: 34: 35).
Cont on sts as set, working in patt from chart, rep the 24 row patt throughout.
Work until 36 (36: 38: 40: 40: 40) rows in all completed (ending with the same patt row as back and front to beg of raglan shaping), ending with a WS row.
Shape raglan
Cast off 5 sts at beg of next 2 rows.
70 (72: 74: 76: 78: 80) sts.
XS, S, M, L, & XL sizes only:
Dec 1 st at each end of next 7 (7: 7: 5: 3: -) rows. 56 (58: 60: 66: 72: -) sts.
Work 1 row.

XXL size only:
Work 2 rows.
All sizes:
Dec 1 st at each end of next row and every foll alt row until 46 (48: 50: 52: 54: 56) sts rem, ending with a **RS** row.
Work 1 row.
Cast off, taking 2 sts together over cables.

Right sleeve
Work as given for left sleeve to ***.
Row 1 (RS): P30 (31: 32: 33: 34: 35), work 20 sts from **chart B** row 1, P30 (31: 32: 33: 34: 35).
Row 2: K30 (31: 32: 33: 34: 35), work 20 sts from **chart B** row 2, K30 (31: 32: 33: 34: 35).
Complete as given for left sleeve.

Making up
Press all pieces using a warm iron over a damp cloth.
Join three raglan seams using back stitch or mattress st if preferred, leaving the left back seam open.
Neck edging
With RS of left sleeve top facing, and using a 4 ½ mm (US 7) circular needle, pick up and knit 40 (42: 44: 46: 48: 50) sts across left sleeve top, place a marker on needle and another half way across sleeve sts, 56 (58: 60: 62: 64: 66) sts across front neck place a marker on needle, 40 (42: 44: 46: 48: 50) sts across right sleeve top, place a marker on needle and another half way across sleeve sts, and 56 (58: 60: 62: 64: 66) sts across back neck.
192 (200: 208: 216: 224: 232) sts.

Next row (WS): (Knit to next marker, slip marker from left to right needle) to end.
Cont in garter st i.e. K every row, taking markers up the knitting, and shape neck as folls:
Work 2 (2: 2: 4: 4: 4) rows.
Next row (RS)(dec): K2, K2tog tbl, * K to 3 sts before next marker, K2tog, K2, K2tog tbl; rep from * 5 times more, K to last 4 sts, K2tog, K2. 180 (188: 196: 204: 212: 220) sts.
Work 3 rows.
Rep the last 4 rows once more, and then the dec row again, ending with a **RS** row.
156 (164: 172: 180: 188: 196) sts.
Change to 4 mm (US 6) circular needle.
Work 3 rows, ending with a WS row.
Work the dec row once more.
144 (152: 160: 168: 176: 184) sts.
Work 2 rows.
Cast off knitwise (on WS), casting off quite firmly over sleeve tops.
Join rem raglan seam and neck edging seam.
Join side and sleeve seams.

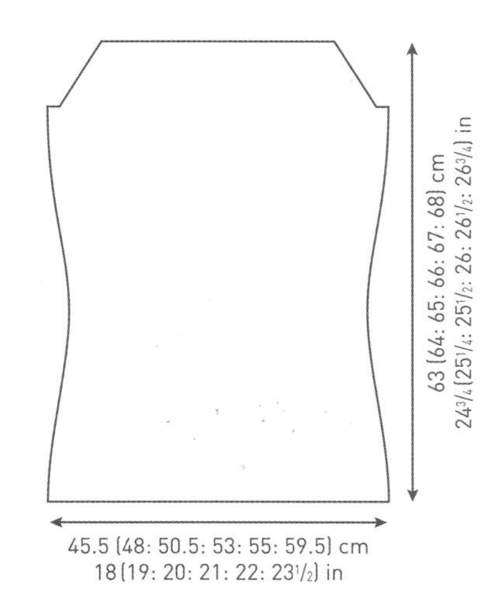

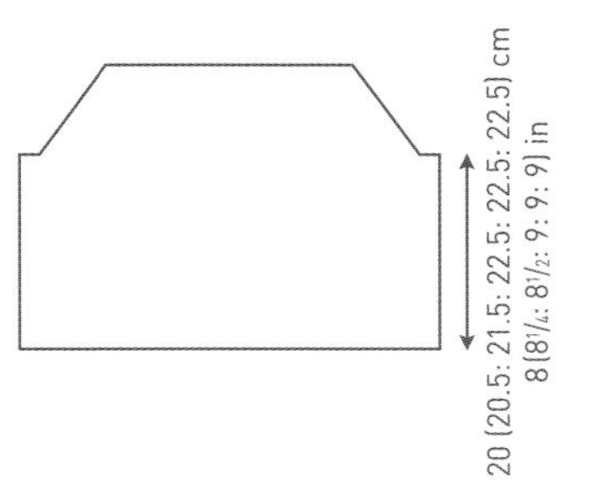

Please Note: These measurements do not include the neck edging.

ChartB

24

20

10

24 row rep

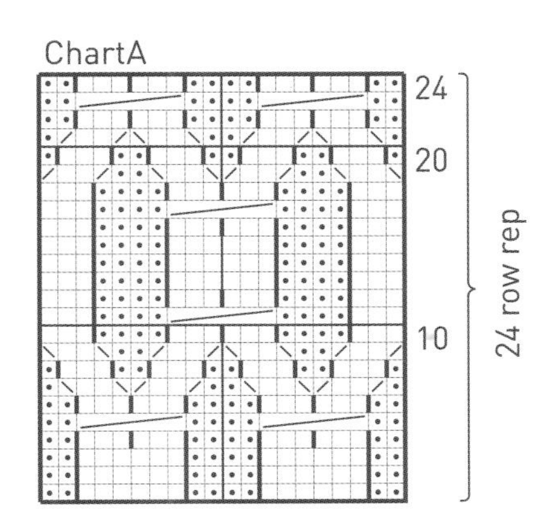

Key

K on RS, P on WS

P on RS, K on WS

Slip 2 sts onto cn, hold at back, K2, K2 from cn.

Slip 2 sts onto cn, hold at front, K2, K2 from cn.

Slip 1 st onto cn, hold at back, K2, P1 from cn.

Slip 2 sts onto cn, hold at front, P1, K2 from cn.

TENDER

CARDIGAN WITH FLOUNCE EDGING AND GARTER STITCH TRIM

Recommendation
Suitable for the knitter with a little experience
Please see page 42 for photograph.

	XS	S	M	L	XL	XXL	
To fit	**81**	**86**	**91**	**97**	**102**	**107**	**cm**
bust	32	34	36	38	40	42	in

Rowan Kidsilk Haze
Photographed in Smoke

5	5	6	6	7	7	x50gm

Needles
1 pair 2¾ mm (no 12) (US 2) needles
1 pair 3¼ mm (no 10) (US 3) needles

Buttons · 5

Tension
25 sts and 34 rows to 10 cm measured over pattern using 3¼ mm (US 3) needles.

BACK
Cast on 272 (284: 304: 316: 340: 364) sts using 3¼ mm (US 3) needles and work lower frill as folls:
Row 1 (RS) (dec): *K2 sts, lift the 1st st over the 2nd st (1 st decreased); rep from * to end. 136 (142: 152: 158: 170: 182) sts.
Row 2: Purl.
Beg with a K row cont in st st as folls:
Work 24 (24: 26: 26: 28: 28) rows, ending with a WS row.
Change to 2¾ mm (US 2) needles
XS, S & XL sizes only
Next row (RS)(dec): K5 (8: 9), (K3tog, K3, K3tog, K4) 9 (9: 11) times, K3tog, K3, K3tog, K5 (8: 9). 96 (102: 122) sts.
M, L & XXL sizes only
Next row (RS)(dec): K6 (9: 8), (K3tog, K4, K3tog, K3) 10 (10: 12) times, K3tog, K4, K3tog,K6 (9: 8). 108 (114: 130) sts.
Knit 5 (5: 5: 7: 7: 7) rows, end with a WS row.
Change to 3¼ mm (US 3) needles
Beg with a K row, work 14 rows in st st, ending with a WS row.
Next row (RS) (inc): K2, M1, K to last 2 sts, M1, K2. 98 (104: 110: 116: 124: 132) sts.
Work 9 rows.
Inc 1 st as before at each end of next and every foll 10th row to 108 (114: 118: 124: 130: 138) sts, and then for **M, L, XL & XXL sixes only** every foll 12th row to 120 (126: 134: 142) sts.
Work straight until back measures 23.5 (23.5: 24.5: 24.5: 24.5: 24.5) cm from top of frill, ending with a WS row.
Shape armholes
Cast off 5 sts at beg of next 2 rows.
98 (104: 110: 116: 124: 132) sts.
Dec 1 st at each end of next 7 (7: 7: 7: 9: 9) rows, then on 2 (3: 4: 5: 4: 5) foll alt rows, and then on foll 4th row. 78 (82: 86: 90: 96: 102) sts.
Work straight until armhole measures 18 (19: 19: 20: 21: 22) cm, ending with a WS row.
Shape shoulders and back neck
Cast off 5 (5: 6: 6: 7: 8) sts at beg of next 2 rows.
Cast off 5 (5: 5: 6: 7: 7) sts, K until 8 (9: 9: 10: 10: 11) sts on right needle and turn, leaving rem sts on a holder. Work each side of neck separately.
Cast off 4 sts, work to end.
Cast off rem 4 (5: 5: 6: 6: 7) sts.
With RS facing rejoin yarn to rem sts, cast off centre 42 (44: 46: 46: 48: 50) sts, work to end.
Complete to match fi rst side, reversing shaping.

LEFT FRONT
Cast on 142 (148: 158: 164: 176: 188) sts using 3¼ mm (US 3) needles and work lower frill as folls:
Row 1 (RS) (dec): *K2 sts, lift the 1st st over the 2nd st (1 st decreased); rep from * to end. 71 (74: 79: 82: 88: 94) sts.
Row 2: K12, P to end.
Row 3: Knit.
Row 4: Work as row 2.
The last 2 rows set the sts, i.e. 12 sts at centre front in garter stitch for front band and rem sts worked in st st.
Work 22 (22: 24: 24: 26: 26) rows, ending with a WS row.
Change to 2¾ mm (US 2) needles
XS, S & XL sizes only
Next row (RS)(dec): K5 (8: 9), (K3tog, K3, K3tog, K4) 3 (3: 4) times, K3tog, K3, K3tog, K to end.
55 (58: 68) sts.
M, L & XXL sizes only
Next row (RS)(dec): K6 (9: 8), (K3tog, K4, K3tog, K3) 4 (4: 5) times, K3tog, K to end.
61 (64: 72) sts.
Knit 5 (5: 5: 7: 7: 7) rows, place a button marker on the 4th of these rows, and end with a WS row.
Change to 3¼ mm (US 3) needles
Working 12 sts at centre front in garter stitch and rem sts in st st, cont as folls:
Work 14 rows in st st, ending with a WS row.
Next row (RS) (inc): K2, M1, K to end.
Work 9 rows.

Inc 1 st as before at beg of next and every foll 10th row to 61 (64: 66: 69: 72: 76) sts, and then for **M, L, XL & XXL sixes only** every foll 12th row to 67 (70: 74: 78) sts.
Work straight until left front matches back to beg of armhole shaping, ending with a WS row.

Shape armhole

Cast off 5 sts at beg of next row.
56 (59: 62: 65: 69:73) sts.
Work 1 row.
Dec 1 st at armhole edge on next 7 (7: 7: 7: 9: 9) rows, then on 2 (3: 4: 5: 4: 5) foll alt rows, and then on foll 4th row.
46 (48: 50: 52: 55: 58) sts.
Work straight until front is 20 (20: 20: 20: 22: 22) rows shorter than back to beg of shoulder shaping, ending with a WS row.

Shape front neck

Next row (RS): Knit 25 (26: 27: 29: 33: 35) sts and turn, leaving rem 21 (22: 23: 23: 22: 23) sts on a holder for neckband.
Dec 1 st at neck edge on next 6 (6: 6: 6: 8: 8) rows, then on 4 foll alt rows, and then on foll 4th row. 14 (15: 16: 18: 20: 22) sts.
Work 1 row, ending with a WS row.

Shape shoulder

Cast off 5 (5: 6: 6: 7: 8) sts at beg of next row and 5 (5: 5: 6: 7: 7) sts at beg of foll alt row.
Work 1 row.
Cast off rem 4 (5: 5: 6: 6: 7) sts.
Mark the position of 5 buttons, the first to come at the waist on the 4th row of garter stitch (previously marked), the 5th to come 4 rows down from beg of front neck shaping and the rem 3 spaced evenly between.

RIGHT FRONT

Cast on 142 (148: 158: 164: 176: 188) sts using 3¼ mm (US 3) needles and work lower frill as folls:
Row 1 (RS) (dec): *K2 sts, lift the 1st st over the 2nd st (1 st decreased); rep from * to end.
71 (74: 79: 82: 88: 94) sts.
Row 2: P to last 12 sts, K12.
Row 3: Knit.
Row 4: Work as row 2.
The last 2 rows set the sts, i.e. 12 sts at centre front in garter stitch for front band and rem sts worked in st st.
Work 22 (22: 24: 24: 26: 26) rows, ending with a WS row.
Change to 2¾ mm (US 2) needles

XS, S & XL sizes only

Next row (RS)(dec): K18, (K3tog, K3, K3tog, K4) 3 (3: 4) times, K3tog, K3, K3tog, K to end.
55 (58: 68) sts.

M, L & XXL sizes only

Next row (RS)(dec): K18, (K3tog, K4, K3tog, K3) 4 (4: 5) times, K3tog, K to end. 61 (64: 72) sts.
Knit 3 rows, ending with a WS row.
Next row (RS)(buttonhole): K5, cast off 3, K to end.
Next row: Knit, casting on 3 sts over those cast off on previous row.
Knit 0 (0: 0: 2: 2: 2) rows, ending with a WS row.
Change to 3¼ mm (US 3) needles
Working 12 sts at centre front in garter stitch with rem sts in st st and working a further 4 buttonholes to correspond with button markers on left front, complete to match left front reversing shaping.

SLEEVES (both alike)

Cast on 100 (108: 112: 116: 124: 128) sts using 3¼ mm (US 3) needles.
Row 1 (RS) (dec): *K2 sts, lift the 1st st over the 2nd st (1 st decreased); rep from * to end.
50 (54: 56: 58: 62: 64) sts.
Row 2: Purl.
Beg with a K row, cont in st st as folls:
Work 28 rows, ending with a WS row.
Next row (RS)(inc): K2, M1, K to last 2 sts, M1, K2.
52 (56: 58: 60: 64: 66) sts.
Work 9 rows.
Inc 1 st as before at each end of next row and every foll 10th row to 74 (78: 80: 82: 74: 76) sts and then for **XL & XXL sizes only** every foll 12th row to 86 (88) sts.
74 (78: 80: 82: 86: 88) sts.
Work straight until sleeve measures 45 (46: 47: 48: 49: 50) cm, ending with a WS row.

Shape sleeve top

Cast off 5 sts at beg of next 2 rows.
64 (68: 70: 72: 76: 78) sts.
Dec 1 st at each end of next 3 rows, then on foll 2 alt rows, and then on every foll 4th row to 42 (46: 48: 50: 54: 56) sts, ending with a **RS** row.
Work 1 row.
Dec 1 st at each end of next row and 3 (4: 4: 5: 6: 6) foll alt rows and then on every foll row to 24 (26: 28: 28: 30: 28) sts.
Cast off.

MAKING UP

Pin the pieces out, pulling gently to the correct size and shape. Using a steam iron, steam the pieces, but **do** not let the iron touch the knitting at all. Leave for a few seconds to cool, then complete as folls:
Join the shoulders seams using back stitch or mattress stitch if preferred.

Neck edging

With RS of right front facing and using 2¾ mm (US 2) slip 21 (22: 23: 23: 22: 23) sts on a holder onto the right needle, pick up and knit 24 (24: 24: 24: 26: 26) sts up right front neck, 50 (52: 54: 54: 56: 58) sts across back and 24 (24: 24: 24: 26: 26) sts down left front, K across 21 (22: 23: 23: 22: 23) sts on holder.
140 (144: 148: 148: 152: 156) sts.
Knit 8 rows, ending with a **RS** row.
Cast off knitwise on wrong side.
Join sleeve and side seams.
Set sleeve top into armhole.
Sew on buttons to correspond with buttonholes.

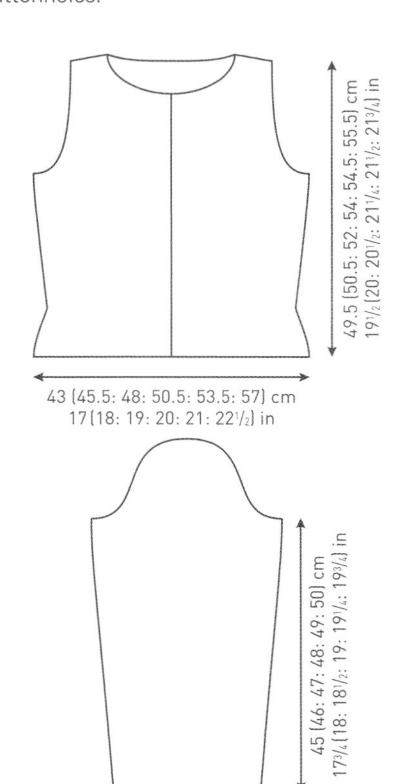

ENCHANT

SHORT SLEEVED SHRUG WORKED FROM CUFF TO CUFF

Recommendation
Suitable for the knitter with a little experience
Please see page 44 for photograph.

	XS	S	M	L	XL	XXL	
To fit	**81**	**86**	**91**	**97**	**102**	**107**	**cm**
bust	32	34	36	38	40	42	in

Rowan Calmer
Photographed in Plum

5	5	6	6	7	8	x50gm

Needles
1 pair 4 mm (no 8) (US 6) needles
1 pair 5 mm (no 6) (US 8) needles

Tension
21 sts and 30 rows to 10 cm measured over stocking stitch using 5 mm (US 8) needles.

Special abbreviations
MP = Make picot, cast on 1 st, cast off 1 st.

MAIN KNITTING (knitted from right cuff to left cuff)
Right sleeve
Cast on 72 (74: 76: 78: 80: 82) sts using 5 mm (US 8) needles and beg with a K row cont in st st as folls:
Work 10 (12: 12: 14: 14: 14) rows, ending with a WS row.
Next row (RS)(inc): K2, M1, K to last 2 sts, M1, K2. 74 (76: 78: 80: 82: 84) sts.
Work 9 (9: 9: 11: 11: 11) rows.
Inc 1 st as before at each end of next row, and then on foll 10th row.
78 (80: 82: 84: 86: 88) sts.
L, XL & XXL sizes only:
Work 0 (0: 0: 3: 5: 7) rows, ending with a WS row.
Inc 1 st as before at each end of next row.
78 (80: 82: 86: 88: 90) sts.
All sizes:
Work 1 row, ending with a WS row.
Shape side
Inc 1 st at each end of next row and 3 (3: 4: 1: 2: 2) foll alt rows.
86 (88: 92: 90: 94: 96) sts.
Work 1 row, ending with a WS row.
Cast on 3 (4: 5: 2: 2: 3) sts at beg of next 2 rows and 6 sts at beg of next 8 (8: 8: 10: 10: 10) rows, ending with a WS row.
140 (144: 150: 154: 158: 162) sts.
Work right front and back
Work 23 (25: 29: 33: 33: 35) rows, ending with a **RS** row.
Shape lower right front
Dec 1 st at end of next row and 3 (2: 3: 3: 4: 4) foll alt rows.
136 (141: 146: 150: 153: 157) sts.
Divide for neck
Next row (RS) (dec): K until 56 (60: 60: 62: 65: 67) sts on right needle and turn, leaving rem sts on a holder for back.
Work back and front separately.
Next row (WS): Cast off 5 (5: 5: 6: 4: 4) sts at beg and dec 1 st at end of row.
50 (54: 54: 55: 60: 62) sts.
Work 1 row.
Cast off 3 sts at beg and dec 1 st at end of next row and 2 (3: 3: 2: 2: 2) foll alt rows.
38 (38: 38: 43: 48: 50) sts.
Next row (RS)(dec): Dec 1 st, work to end.
Next row: Cast off 3 sts at beg and dec 1 st at end of row.
33 (33: 33: 38: 43: 45) sts.
Rep the last 2 rows 1 (1: 1: 2: 3: 3) times more. 28 (28: 28: 28: 28: 30) sts.
Cast off 3 sts at beg of next 4 rows.
16 (16: 16: 16: 16: 18) sts.
Cast off.
With RS facing rejoin yarn to rem 80 (81: 86: 88: 88: 90) sts, cast off centre 11 (10: 12: 12: 10: 10) sts, K to end.
69 (71: 74: 76: 78: 80) sts.
Dec 1 st at neck edge on next 4 rows, ending with a **RS** row.
65 (67: 70: 72: 74: 76) sts.
Work 39 (41: 41: 43: 43: 47) rows, ending with a WS row.
Inc 1 st at neck edge on next 4 rows, ending with a WS row.
69 (71: 74: 76: 78: 80) sts.
Leave sts on a spare needle.
Left front
Cast on 16 (16: 16: 16: 16: 18) sts using 5 mm (US 8) needles and beg with a K row cont in st st as folls:
Work 1 row.
Cast on 3 sts at beg of next 4 rows.
28 (28: 28: 28: 28: 30) sts.
Next row (WS): Cast on 3 sts at beg and inc 1 st at end of row.
Next row: Inc 1 st, work to end.
33 (33: 33: 33: 33: 35) sts.
Rep the last 2 rows 1 (1: 1: 2: 3: 3) times more. 38 (38: 38: 43: 48: 50) sts.
Cast on 3 sts at beg and inc 1 st at end of next row and 2 (3: 3: 2: 2: 2) foll alt rows.
50 (54: 54: 55: 60: 62) sts.
Work 1 row.
Next row (WS): Cast on 5 (5: 5: 6: 4: 4) sts at beg and inc 1 st at end of row.
56 (60: 60: 62: 65: 67)sts.

Join front and back together

Next row (RS): K56 (60: 60: 62: 65: 67) sts, cast on 11 (10: 12: 12: 10: 10) sts, K across 69 (71: 74: 76: 78: 80) sts on spare needle. 136 (141: 146: 150: 153: 157) sts.

Inc 1 st at end of next row and foll 3 (2: 3: 3: 4: 4) alt rows. 140 (144: 150: 154: 158: 162) sts.

Work 24 (26: 30: 34: 34: 36) rows, ending with a WS row.

Shape sides

Cast off 6 sts at beg of next 8 (8: 8: 10: 10: 10) rows, and then 3 (4: 5: 2: 2: 3) sts at beg of next 2 rows. 86 (88: 92: 90: 94: 96) sts.

Next row (RS) (dec): K2, K2tog, K to last 4 sts, K2tog tbl, K2. 84 (86: 90: 88: 92: 94) sts.

Work 1 row.

Dec 1 st at each end of next row and 3 (3: 4: 1: 2: 2) foll alt rows. 76 (78: 80: 84: 86: 88) sts.

L, XL & XXL sizes only:

Work 0 (0: 0: 3: 5: 7) rows, end with a WS row.

Dec 1 st as before at each end of next row, end with a WS row. 76 (78: 80: 82: 84: 86) sts.

All sizes:

Work 9 rows.

Dec 1 st as before at each end of next row, and then on foll 10th (10th: 10th: 12th: 12th: 12th) row. 72 (74: 76: 78: 80: 82) sts.

Work 9 (11: 11: 13: 13: 13) rows, ending with a WS row.

Cast off.

MAKING UP

Press knitting using a warm iron over a damp cloth.

Join underarm and side seams preferably using mattress st.

Front edging

Cast on 14 (15: 15: 16: 16: 17) sts using 4 mm (US 6) needles.

Row 1 (RS): MP, knit to end.

Row 2: Purl.

Row 3: MP, purl to end.

Row 4: Knit.

These 4 rows form the patt and are rep throughout.

Cont in pattern until edging fits neatly and **not stretched** from right side seam around front curve and up front to shoulder, across back neck, down and around left front to left side seam and across lower back to right side seam. Slip stitch neatly into place, **stretching** edging slightly across lower back, adjusting length if necessary.

Cast off.

Join ends of edging neatly together.

Cuffs (make 2)

Cast on 14 (15: 15: 16: 16: 17) sts using 4 mm (US 6) needles.

Row 1 (RS): MP, knit to end.

Row 2: Purl.

Row 3: MP, purl to end.

Row 4: Knit.

These 4 rows form the patt and are rep throughout.

Work until 23 (24: 25: 26: 26: 27) patt reps in all completed, ending with a WS row.

Work 2 more rows.

Cast off.

Join seam.

Stitch the straight edge of the cuff neatly into place around lower edge of sleeve, stretching the cuff to fit the sleeve.

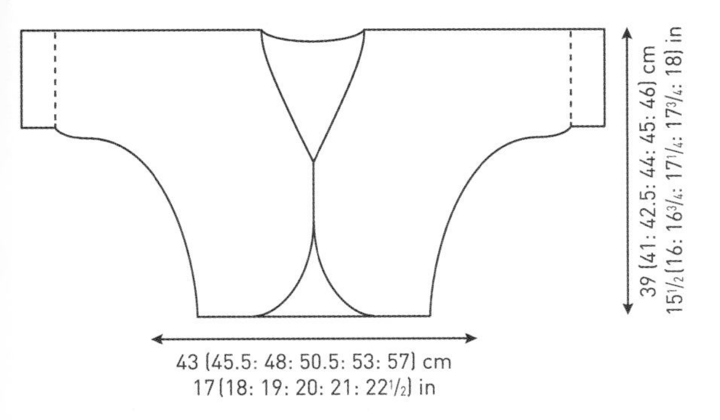

JASMINE

NEAT SWEATER WITH GARTER STITCH YOKE & BUTTON DETAIL

Recommendation
Suitable for the knitter with a little experience
Please see pages 46 – 49 for photographs.

	XS	S	M	L	XL	XXL	
To fit	**81**	**86**	**91**	**97**	**102**	**109**	**cm**
bust	32	34	36	38	40	43	in

Rowan 4 ply cotton
Photographed in Shale

5	5	6	6	7	8	x50gm

Buttons - 6 (6: 6: 6: 7: 7)

Needles
1 pair 2 ¼ mm (no 13) (US 1) needles
1 pair 2 ¾ mm (no 12) (US 2) needles
1 2 ¼ mm (no 13) (US 1) circular needle

Tension
28 sts and 38 rows to 10 cm measured over **stocking stitch** using 2 ¾ mm (US 2) needles.
28 sts and 44 rows to 10cm measured over **garter stitch** using 2 ¾ mm (US 2) needles

BACK
Cast on 113 (117: 123: 129: 137: 147) sts using 2 ¼ mm (US 1) needles and work lower edging as folls:
Knit 3 rows, ending with a **RS** row.
Next row (WS): K1, (P1, K1) to end.
Next row: K1, (P1, K1) to end.
These 2 rows form moss st.
Work 9 (9: 13: 13: 13: 13) more rows in moss st, ending with a WS row.
Change to 2 ¾ mm (US 2) needles and beg with a K row cont in st st, shaping sides as folls:
Next row (RS)(dec): K2, K2tog, K to last 4 sts, K2tog tbl, K2.
111 (115: 121: 127: 135: 145) sts.
Work 7 rows.
Dec 1 st as before at each end of next row and 3 foll 8th rows, and then on the foll 6th row.
101 (105: 111: 117: 125: 135) sts.
Work 13 rows straight, ending with a WS row.
Next row (RS)(inc): K2, M1, K to last 2 sts, M1, K2.
Work 9 rows.
Inc 1 st as before at each end of next row, then on every foll 10th row to 117 (121: 127: 133: 141: 151) sts, ending with a **RS** row.
Work straight until back measures 39 (39: 40: 40: 40: 40) cm from cast on edge, ending with a WS row.
Now cont in **garter st** i.e. knit every row, and shape raglans as folls:
Shape raglans
Cast off 8 (8: 8: 9: 10: 12) sts at beg of next 2 rows.
101 (105: 111: 115: 121: 127) sts. **
Knit 2 rows.
Next row (RS)(dec): K3, K2tog, K to last 5 sts, K2tog tbl, K3.
99 (103: 109: 113: 119: 125) sts.
Knit 3 rows.
Dec 1 st as before at each end of next row and every foll 4th row to 83 (83: 93: 93: 99: 103) sts, and then on every foll alt row until 67 (71: 73: 77: 79: 83) sts, ending with a **RS** row.
Work 1 row.
Cast off.

Front
Work as given for back to **.
Divide for front neck
Next row (RS): K47 (49: 52: 54: 57: 60) sts, and leave these on a holder for left front, K to end.
54 (56: 59: 61: 64: 67) sts.
Work each side of neck separately.
Knit 1 row.
XS size only:
Row 1 (RS)(dec)(buttonhole): K2, K2tog, yon, K3, yon, K2tog tbl (this forms the eyelet edging to buttonhole band), K to last 5 sts, K2tog tbl, K3. 53 sts.
Row 2: Knit 1 row.
Row 3 (RS): K7, yon, K2tog tbl, K to end.
Row 4: Knit 1 row.
S & M sizes only:
Row 1 (RS)(dec): K7, yon, K2tog tbl (this forms the eyelet edging to buttonhole band), K to last 5 sts, K2tog tbl, K3. (55: 58) sts.
Rows 2, 4 & 6: Knit 1 row.
Row (RS): K7, yon, K2tog tbl, K to end.
Row 5 (RS)(dec)(buttonhole): K2, K2tog, yon, K3, yon, K2tog tbl (this forms the eyelet edging to buttonhole band), K to last 5 sts, K2tog tbl, K3.
(54: 57) sts.
Row 7: K7, yon, K2tog tbl, K to end.
Row 8: Knit 1 row.
L size only:
Row 1(RS)(dec): K7, yon, K2tog tbl (this forms the eyelet edging to buttonhole band), K to last 5 sts, K2tog tbl, K3.
(60) sts.
Rows 2, 4 & 6: Knit 1 row.
Row 3 (RS): K7, yon, K2tog tbl, K to end.
Row 5 (RS)(dec): K7, yon K2tog tbl, K to last 5 sts, K2tog tbl, K3. (59) sts.
Row 7 (RS)(buttonhole): K2, K2tog, yon, K3, yon, K2tog tbl, K to end.
Row 8: Knit 1 row.
XL & XXL sizes only:
Row 1 (RS)(dec): K7, yon, K2tog tbl (this forms the eyelet edging to buttonhole band), K to last 5 sts, K2tog tbl, K3.
(63: 66) sts.

Rows 2, 4 & 6: Knit 1 row.
Row 3 (RS) (buttonhole): K2, K2tog, yon, K3, yon, K2tog tbl, K to end.
Row 5 (RS)(dec): K7, yon, K2tog tbl, K to last 5 sts, K2tog tbl, K3. (62: 65) sts.
Row 7 (RS): K7, yon, K2tog tbl, K to end.
Row 8: Knit 1 row.
All sizes:
Keeping eyelet patt correct up entire front edge, cont dec 1 st as before on next row and 7 (7: 6: 8: 8: 9) foll 4th rows, and then on 1 (0: 3: 0: 2: 0) foll alt rows, and **at the same time** work 4 (4: 4: 4: 5: 5) more buttonholes each worked 8 rows from last, ending with a **RS** row.
44 (46: 47: 50: 51: 55) sts.
Knit 1 (3: 1: 1: 1: 1) rows.
Shape front neck
Next row (RS): K7, yon, K2tog tbl, K until 31 (33: 34: 34: 36: 35) sts on right needle, and leave these on a holder for neck edging, K to last 5 sts, K2tog tbl, K3.
12 (12: 12: 15: 14: 19) sts.
Cont dec 1 st as before as raglan edge and **at the same time** dec 1 st at neck edge on every row until 3 (3: 3: 3: 5: 7) sts rem.
Dec 1 st at neck edge on every row until 1 st rems.
Fasten off.
With **WS** facing, rejoin yarn to 47 (49: 52: 54: 57: 60) sts on holder for left front and work as folls:
Cast on 7 sts, patt to end.
54 (56: 59: 61: 64: 67) sts.
Complete to match first side, reversing all shapings, omitting buttonholes and working the eyelet patt as folls: K to last 9 sts, K2tog, yon, K7.

Sleeves (both alike)
Cast on 79 (81: 83: 87: 89: 95) sts using 2 ¼ mm (US 1) needles and work lower edging as folls:
Knit 3 rows, ending with a **RS** row.
Next row (WS): K1, (P1, K1) to end.
Next row: K1, (P1, K1) to end.
These 2 rows form moss st.
Work 1 (1: 3: 3: 5: 5) more rows in moss st, ending with a WS row.
Change to 2 ¾ mm (US 2) needles and cont in garter st, i.e. knit every row, and shape raglans as folls:

Shape raglans
Cast off 8 (8: 8: 9: 10: 12) sts at beg of next 2 rows. 63 (65: 67: 69: 69: 71) sts.
Knit 4 (4: 4: 4: 6: 6) rows, ending with a WS row.
Next row (RS)(dec): K3, K2tog, K to last 5 sts, K2tog tbl, K3.
Knit 5 (5: 5: 5: 7: 7) rows.
Dec 1 st as before as each end of next row and 3 (5: 5: 7: 1: 3) foll 6th (6th: 6th: 6th: 8th: 8th) rows and then on 4 (2: 2: 0: 6: 4) foll 4th (4th: 4th: 4th: 6th: 6th) rows, ending with a **RS** row. 45 (47: 49: 51: 51: 53) sts.
Shape left sleeve top
Knit 2 (2: 2: 2: 0: 0) rows.
Next row (WS): Cast off 14 (15: 16: 16: 17: 17) sts, K to end.
Knit 1 row, dec 1 st as before at beg of next row on **XS, S, M & L sizes only.**
30 (31: 32: 34: 34: 36) sts.
Cast off 15 (15: 16: 17: 17: 18) sts, K to end.
Knit 1 row.
Cast off rem 15 (16: 16: 17: 17: 18) sts.
Shape right sleeve top
Knit 3 (3: 3: 3: 1: 1) rows.
Cast off 14 (15: 16: 16: 17: 17) sts at beg of next row and dec 1 st as before at end of row on **XS, S, M & L sizes only.**
30 (31: 32: 34: 34: 36) sts.
Knit 1 row.
Cast off 15 (15: 16: 17: 17: 18) sts, K to end.
Knit 1 row.
Cast off rem 15 (16: 16: 17: 17: 18) sts.

Making up
Press all pieces using a warm iron over a damp cloth.
Join raglan seams using back stitch or preferably mattress st.
Neck edging
With RS of right front facing and using a 2 ¼ mm (US 1) circular needle, slip 31 (33: 34: 34: 36: 35) sts from holder onto needle, rejoin yarn and pick up and knit 8 (8: 8: 10: 10: 14) sts up right front neck, 42 (44: 46: 48: 50: 52) sts across right sleeve top, now place markers on the needle at each side of sleeve stitches and another halfway across sleeve top, 65 (69: 71: 75: 77: 81) sts across back neck, 42 (44: 46: 48: 50: 52) sts across left sleeve top, placing 3 markers as before, and 8 (8: 8: 10: 10: 14) sts down left front neck, K 31 (33: 34: 34: 36: 35) sts from holder on left front. 227 (239: 247: 259: 269: 283) sts.

Keeping eyelet patt correct, cont in garter st as folls:
Knit 1 row.
Next row (RS)(dec): K7, yon, K2tog tbl, *K to 4 sts before next marker, K2tog tbl, K4, K2tog; rep from * 5 times more, knit to last 9 sts, K2tog, yon, K7.
215 (227: 235: 247: 257: 271) sts.
Keeping eyelet patt correct, work 3 rows.
Rep the last 4 rows once more, and at the same time work a buttonhole as before on the next row, ending with a WS row.
203 (215: 223: 235: 245: 259) sts.
Next row (RS)(dec): K7, yon, K2tog tbl, *K to 4 sts before next marker, K2tog tbl, K4, K2tog; rep from * 5 times more, knit to last 9 sts, K2tog, yon, K 7.
191 (203: 211: 223: 233: 247) sts.
Cast off knitwise (on WS), casting off quite firmly over the sleeve top sts.
Join side and sleeve seams. Sew cast-on sts at base of left front opening in place behind right front opening edge.
Press seams and sew on buttons.

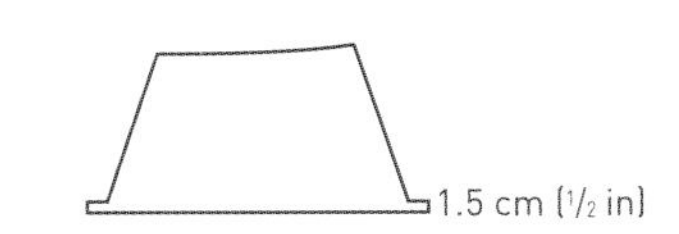

GLISTEN

FITTED BEADED WAISTCOAT

Recommendation
Suitable for the more experienced knitter
Please see page 45 for photograph.

	XS	S	M	L	XL	XXL	
To fit	**81**	**86**	**91**	**97**	**102**	**107**	**cm**
bust	32	34	36	38	40	42	in

Rowan 4 ply cotton
Photographed in Aubergine

4	5	5	6	6	7	x50gm

Beads - Approx 1000 (1100: 1200: 1250: 1300: 1400) x 0.8

Buttons - 6

Needles
1 pair 2 ¼ mm (no 13) (US 1) needles
1 pair 2 ¾ mm (no 12) (US 2) needles

Tension
28 sts and 39 rows to 10 cm measured over beaded stocking stitch using 2 ¾ mm (US 2) needles.

Special abbreviations
Cluster 2 = Bring a bead up to knitting, yrn, P2, holding the bead to the front of the work, lift the yrn over last 2 sts and off RH needle.

Beading note
At the place indicated, thread beads onto yarn. To do this, thread a fine sewing needle (one you will easily pass through the beads) with sewing thread. Knot ends of thread and then pass end of yarn through this loop. Thread a bead onto sewing thread and then gently slide it along and onto knitting yarn. Continue in this way until required number of beads are on yarn.

Underarm edging for left side of back
Cast on 5 (5: 6: 6: 7: 7) sts using 2 3/4 mm (US 2) needles and work as folls:
Row 1 (RS): K1 (1: 0: 0: 1: 1), (P1, K1) to end.
Row 2: (P1, K1) to last 1 (1: 0: 0: 1: 1), P1 (1: 0: 0: 1: 1).
Row 3: P1 (1: 0: 0: 1: 1), (K1, P1) to end.
Row 4: (K1, P1) to last 1 (1: 0: 0: 1: 1), K1 (1: 0: 0: 1: 1).
Rep the last 4 rows until 22 (22: 24: 24: 26: 26) rows in all completed, ending with a WS row.
Leave sts on a holder.

Underarm edging for right side of back
Cast on 5 (5: 6: 6: 7: 7) sts using 2 3/4 mm (US 2) needles and work as folls:
Row 1 (RS): (K1, P1) to last 1 (1: 0: 0: 1: 1), K1 (1: 0: 0: 1: 1).
Row 2: P1 (1: 0: 0: 1: 1), (K1, P1) to end.
Row 3: (P1, K1) to last 1 (1: 0: 0: 1: 1), P1 (1: 0: 0: 1: 1).
Row 4: K1 (1: 0: 0: 1: 1), (P1, K1) to end.
Rep the last 4 rows until 21 (21: 23: 23: 25: 25) rows in all completed, ending with a **RS** row.
Leave sts on a holder.

Back
Cast on 106 (114: 120: 128: 134: 146) sts using 2 ¼ mm (US 1) needles and work lower edging as folls:
Row 1 (RS): (P1, K1) to end.
Row 2: (K1, P1) to end.
Row 3: Work as row 2.
Row 4: Work as row 1.
Rep these 4 rows until 12 (12: 12: 14: 14: 14) rows in all completed, ending with a WS row.
Change to 2 ¾ mm (US 2) needles.
Next row (RS)(dec): K2tog, K to last 2 sts, K2tog. 104 (112: 118: 126: 132: 144) sts.
Next row: Purl.
Cont in patt from chart for back, rep the 12 row patt throughout, and **at the same time,** cont work shaping as folls:
Chart row 1 (RS): Knit.
Break yarn and thread on the beads (don't be tempted to thread too many because the yarn will get very heavy).
Chart row 2 (WS): P6 (4: 1: 5: 2: 2), * cluster 2, P4; rep from * to last 8 (6: 3: 7: 4: 4) sts, cluster 2, P6 (4: 1: 5: 2: 2).
Chart row 3: Knit.
Chart row 4: Purl.
Chart row 5: K2tog, K to last 2 sts, K2tog. 102 (110: 116: 124: 130: 142) sts.
Cont until chart row 12 completed, dec 1 st as before at each end of chart row 11 and ending with a WS row.
100 (108: 114: 122: 128: 140) sts.
Cont in patt, shaping sides as folls:
Work 4 rows.
Dec 1 st as before at each end of next row and 3 foll 6th rows, and then on foll 4th row.
90 (98: 104: 112: 118: 130) sts.
Work 21 rows, ending with a WS row.
Inc 1 st at each end of next row and 5 foll 8th rows, and then every foll 6th row to 110 (118: 124: 132: 138: 150) sts.
Work straight until back measures 37 (37: 38: 38: 38: 38) cm, ending with a WS row.
Shape armholes
Cast off 8 (8: 8: 9: 9: 10) sts at beg of next 2 rows. 94 (102: 108: 114: 120: 130) sts.
Dec 1 st at each end of next 7 (7: 9: 9: 9: 11) rows, ending with a **RS** row.
80 (88: 90: 96: 102: 108) sts.

Join armhole edgings

With WS of left-hand edging facing, slip 5 (5: 6: 6: 7: 7) sts from holder onto right needle, patt across sts for back and now keeping patt correct work 5 (5: 6: 6: 7: 7) sts from right-hand side edging.

90 (98: 102: 108: 116: 122) sts.

Next row (RS)(dec): Patt 5 (5: 6: 6: 7: 7), K2tog, K to last 7 (7: 8: 8: 9: 9) sts, K2tog tbl, patt to end.

88 (96: 100: 106: 114: 120) sts.

Work 1 row.

Dec 1 st as before at each end of next row and 6 (7: 5: 5: 5: 4) foll alt rows, then on 2 foll 4th rows, and then on foll 6th row.

68 (74: 82: 88: 96: 104) sts.

Work straight until armhole measures 18 (19: 19: 20: 21: 22) cm, ending with a WS row.

Shape shoulders and back neck

Cast off 5 (5: 6: 6: 7: 7) sts, work until 12 (14: 16: 18: 20: 23) sts on right needle and turn leaving rem sts on a holder.

Work each side of neck separately.

Dec 1 st, work to end.

11 (13: 15: 17: 19: 22) sts.

Cast off 5 (6: 7: 8: 9: 11) sts at beg and dec 1 st at end of next row.

5 (6: 7: 8: 9: 10) sts.

Work 1 row.

Cast off.

With RS facing rejoin yarn to rem sts, cast off centre 34 (36: 38: 40: 42: 44) sts, work to end.

Complete to match first side, reversing shaping.

Underarm edging for left front

Work as given for underarm edging for right side of back.

Left front

Cast on 58 (62: 65: 69: 72: 78) sts using 2 ¼ mm (US 1) needles and work lower edging as folls:

Row 1 (RS): K0 (0: 1: 1: 0: 0), (P1, K1) to end.

Row 2: (K1, P1) to last 0 (0: 1: 1: 0: 0) st, K0 (0: 1: 1: 0: 0).

Row 3: P0 (0: 1: 1: 0: 0), (K1, P1) to end.

Row 4: (P1, K1) to last 0 (0: 1: 1: 0: 0) st, P0 (0: 1: 1: 0: 0).

Rep these 4 rows until 12 (12: 12: 14: 14: 14) rows in all completed, ending with a WS row.

Change to 2 ¾ mm (US 2) needles.

Next row (RS)(dec): K2tog, K to last 7 (7: 8: 8: 9: 9) sts, patt to end.

57 (61: 64: 68: 71: 77) sts.

Next row: Patt 7 (7: 8: 8: 9: 9), P to end.

Cont in patt from chart for left front, rep the 12 row patt throughout, and **at the same time,** cont working shaping as folls:

Chart row 1 (RS): K to last 7 (7: 8: 8: 9: 9) sts, patt to end.

Break yarn and thread on the beads (don't be tempted to thread too many because the yarn will get very heavy).

Chart row 2 (WS): Patt 7 (7: 8: 8: 9: 9), P0 (0: 5: 5: 4: 4), * cluster 2, P4; rep from * to last to last 8 (6: 3: 7: 4: 4) sts, cluster 2, P6 (4: 1: 5: 2: 2).

Chart row 3: Work as row 1.

Chart row 4: Patt 7 (7: 8: 8: 9: 9), P to end.

Chart row 5: K2tog, K to last 7 (7: 8: 8: 9: 9) sts, patt to end. 56 (60: 63: 67: 70: 76) sts.

Cont until chart row 12 completed, dec 1 st as before at beg of chart row 11 and ending with a WS row.

55 (59: 62: 66: 69: 75) sts.

Cont in patt, shaping side as folls:

Work 4 rows.

Dec 1 st as before at beg of next row and 3 foll 6th rows, and then on foll 4th row.

50 (54: 57: 61: 64: 70) sts.

Work 21 rows, ending with a WS row.

Shape front neck

Cont shaping at side edge and front neck as folls:

Next row (RS)(inc)(dec): Inc in first st, work to last 9 (9: 10: 10: 11: 11) sts, K2tog tbl, patt to end.

50 (54: 57: 61: 64: 70) sts.

Cont to dec as before at neck edge on every foll 8th row **and at the same time** cont to inc at side edge on 5 foll 8th rows and then on 4 foll 6th rows (as on back).

51 (55: 58: 62: 65: 71) sts.

After completing the last side inc, keeping the front neck shaping correct, work until front matches back to armhole shaping, ending with a WS row.

Shape armhole

Cast off 8 (8: 8: 9: 9: 10) sts at beg of next row.

Work 1 row.

Dec 1 st at armhole edge on next 7 (7: 9: 9: 9: 11) rows, ending with a **RS** row.

Join armhole edgings

Work 1 row, and now keeping patt correct work 5 (5: 6: 6: 7: 7) sts from left-hand side edging.

Next row (RS)(dec): Patt 5 (5: 6: 6: 7: 7), K2tog, patt to end, working neck dec if appropriate.

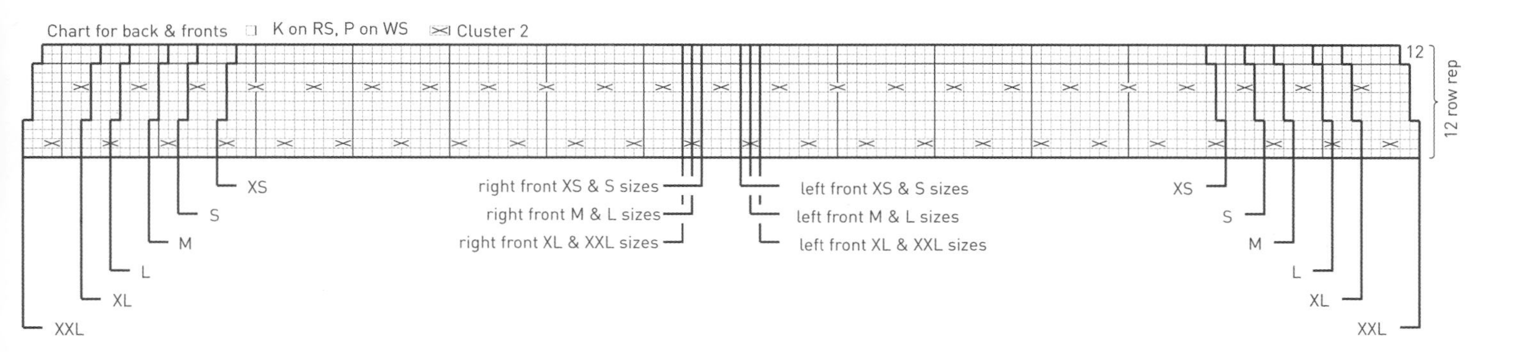

Work 1 row.
Keeping front neck dec correct, dec 1 st as before at armhole edge on next row and 6 (7: 5: 5: 5: 4) foll alt rows, then on 2 foll 4th rows, and then on foll 6th row.
Cont to dec at neck edge until 23 (25: 29: 31: 35: 38) sts rem.
Work straight until front matches back to shape shoulder, ending with a WS row.

Shape shoulder

Cast off 5 (5: 6: 6: 7: 7) sts at beg of next row and 5 (6: 7: 8: 9: 11) sts at beg of foll alt row. 13 (14: 16: 17: 19: 20) sts.
Work 1 row.
Cast off 5 (6: 7: 8: 9: 10) sts (one st on right needle after cast-off), inc in next st, patt to end. 6 (6: 7: 7: 8: 8) sts.
Cont on these sts for a further 6.5 (6.5: 7: 7: 8: 8) cm.
Cast off.
Mark the position of 6 buttons, the first to come in first row after needle change, the 6th 4 rows down from start of front neck shaping and rem 4 spaced evenly between.

Underarm edging for right front

Work as given for underarm edging for left side of back.

Right front

Cast on 58 (62: 65: 69: 72: 78) sts using 2 ¼ mm (US 1) needles and work lower edging as folls:
Row 1 (RS): (K1, P1) to last 0 (0: 1: 1: 0: 0) st, K0 (0: 1: 1: 0: 0).
Row 2: K0 (0: 1: 1: 0: 0), (P1, K1) to end.
Row 3: (P1, K1) to last 0 (0: 1: 1: 0: 0) st, P0 (0: 1: 1: 0: 0).
Row 4: P0 (0: 1: 1: 0: 0), (K1, P1) to end.
Rep these 4 rows until 12 (12: 12: 14: 14: 14) rows in all completed, ending with a WS row.
Change to 2 ¾ mm (US 2) needles.
Next row (RS)(dec)(buttonhole): Patt 2 (2: 3: 3: 4: 4), patt 2tog, yon, patt 3, K to last 2 sts, K2tog. 57 (61: 64: 68: 71: 77) sts.
Next row: P to last 7 (7: 8: 8: 9: 9) sts, patt to end.
Cont in patt from chart for right front, rep the 12 row patt throughout, cont shaping sides as folls and **at the same time** work 5 more buttonholes as before to correspond with button markers.

Chart row 1 (RS): Patt 7 (7: 8: 8: 9: 9), K to end.
Break yarn and thread on the beads (don't be tempted to thread too many because the yarn will get very heavy).
Chart row 2 (WS): P6 (4: 1: 5: 2: 2), *cluster 2, P4; rep from * to last 9 (9: 15: 15: 15: 15) sts, cluster 2, P0 (0: 5: 5: 4: 4), patt to end.
Chart row 3: Work as row 1.
Chart row 4: P to last 7 (7: 8: 8: 9: 9), patt to end.
Chart row 5: Patt 7 (7: 8: 8: 9: 9), K to last 2 sts, K2tog. 56 (60: 63: 67: 70: 76) sts.
Cont until chart row 12 completed, dec 1 st as before at end of chart row 11 and ending with a WS row.
55 (59: 62: 66: 69: 75) sts.
Complete as for left front, working from chart for right front, placing buttonholes as indicated, reversing all shaping and joining in armhole edging as on back.

Making up

Press as described on the information page.
Join the shoulder seams using back st or mattress st if preferred, taking extra care when joining the armhole edging.
Join the side seams.
With RS facing, join the cast-off ends of the neckband together, then neatly stitch into place around back neck.
Sew on buttons.

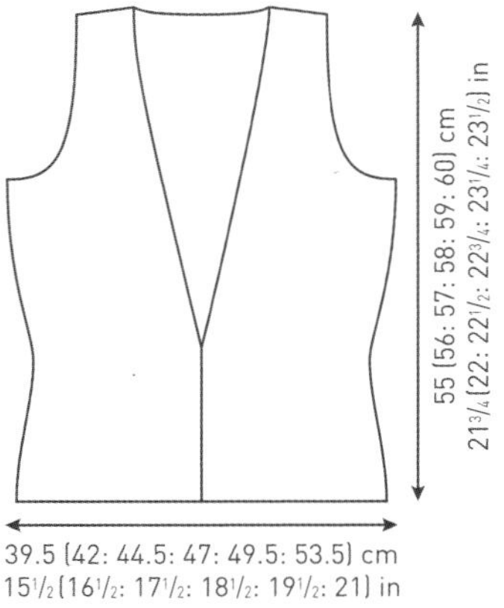

55 [56: 57: 58: 59: 60] cm
21¾ [22: 22½: 22¾: 23¼: 23½] in

39.5 [42: 44.5: 47: 49.5: 53.5] cm
15½ [16½: 17½: 18½: 19½: 21] in

FLICKER

LACY HAT WITH ALL OVER BEADS OR BEADED BAND

Recommendation
Suitable for the knitter with a little experience
Please see pages 38, 39 & 43 for photographs.

Rowan Wool Cotton
Photographed in Tender and Bilberry
2 x 50gm

Needles
1 pair 3mm (no 11) (US 2/3) needles
1 pair 4 mm (no 8) (US 6) needles

To fit: Average size

Beads - approx 400 x 0.6

Tension
21 sts and 27 rows to 10 cm measured over pattern using 4 mm (US 6) needles.

Hat

All over beaded version
Cast on 114 sts using 3mm (US 2/3) needles.
Row 1 (RS): K2, (P2, K2) to end.
Row 2: P2, (K2, P2) to end.
These 2 rows form the rib.
Rep these 2 rows until 15 rows in all have been worked, ending with a **RS** row.
****Next row (WS)(inc):** P1, (M1, rib 4) to last st, M1, P1. 143 sts.
Change to 4 mm (US 6) needles.
Patt note: We know from experience how easy it is to miss the final '(yrn) twice' before the last st, at the end of patt rows 2 and 5.
To avoid loosing stitches, please be aware of this and check your work regularly at these points.
Row 1 (RS): Knit.
Row 2: K1, *sl 1, K2tog, psso, (yrn) twice; rep from * to last st, K1.
Row 3: P1, *P1, K1 into loops made on previous row, P1; rep from * to last st, P1.
Row 4: Knit.
Row 5 (RS): As row 2.
Row 6: As row 3. **
Break yarn.
Thread approx 200 beads onto the new ball of yarn (don't be tempted to thread all the beads at this point because they make the yarn heavy to work with and you may not have sufficient yarn from one ball to place them all.
Row 7 (RS): K2, * bring yarn forward, slip a bead up next to st just worked, slip next st purlwise from left needle to right needle, take yarn back easing the bead into place over the slipped stitch on **RS** of work, K2; rep from * to end.
Rows 2 to 7 form the patt and are repeated.
Rep these last 6 rows 7 times more and then work rows 2 - 3 again, ending with a **RS** row.
*****Next row (WS)(dec):** K2tog, K to last 2 sts, K2tog. 141 sts.

Shape top
Next row (RS)(dec): (K7, K3tog tbl) to last st, K1. 113 sts.
Next row (and every foll WS row): Purl.
Next row (RS)(dec): (K5, K3tog tbl) to last st, K1. 85 sts.
Next row (RS)(dec): (K3, K3tog tbl) to last st, K1. 57 sts.
Next row (RS)(dec): (K1, K3tog tbl) to last st, K1. 29 sts.
Next row (RS)(dec): (K2tog tbl) to last st, K1. 15 sts.
Break yarn and thread through rem 15 sts.
Pull up tight and fasten off securely.
Join seam. ***

Beaded rib version
Thread 392 beads onto yarn.
Cast on 114 sts using 3mm (US 2/3) needles.
Row 1 (RS): K2, * bring yarn forward, slip 2 beads up next to st just worked, slip next 2 sts purlwise from left needle to right needle, take yarn back, K2; rep from * to end.
Row 2: P2, (K2, P2) to end.
Row 3: K2, (P2, K2) to end.
Row 4 (WS): P2, * take yarn back, slip 2 beads up next to st just worked, slip next 2 sts purlwise from left needle to right needle, bring yarn forward, P2; rep from * to end.
Row 5: Work as row 3.
Row 6: Work as row 2.
Rep these 6 rows twice more and then work row 1 again, ending with a **RS** row.
This completes the beading.
Work as given for all over beaded version from ** to **.
The last 6 rows form the patt and are rep throughout.
Rep these 6 rows 7 times more and then work rows 1 – 3 again, ending with a **RS** row.
To complete to hat work as given for all over beaded version from *** to ***.

INFORMATION

A GUIDE TO ASSIST WITH TECHNIQUES & FINISHING TOUCHES

TENSION

Achieving the correct tension has to be one of the most important elements in producing a beautiful, well fitting knitted garment. The tension controls the size and shape of your finished piece and any variation to either stitches or rows, however slight, will affect your work and change the fit completely.
To avoid any disappointment, we would always recommend that you knit a tension square in the yarn and stitch given in the pattern, working perhaps four or five more stitches and rows than those given in the tension note.

When counting the tension, place your knitting on a flat surface and mark out a 10cm square with pins. Count the stitches between the pins. If you have too many stitches to 10cm your knitting it too tight, try again using thicker needles, if you have too few stitches to 10cm your knitting is too loose, so try again using finer needles. Please note, if you are unable to achieve the correct stitches and rows required, the stitches are more crucial as many patterns are knitted to length.
Keep an eye on your tension during knitting, especially if you're going back to work which has been put to one side for any length of time.

SIZING

The instructions are given for the smallest size. Where they vary, work the figures in brackets for the larger sizes. One set of figures refers to all sizes. The size diagram with each pattern will help you decide which size to knit. The measurements given on the size diagram are the actual size your garment should be when completed. Measurements will vary from design to design because the necessary ease allowances have been made in each pattern to give your garment the correct fit, i.e. a loose fitting garment will be several cm wider than a neat fitted one, a snug fitting garment may have no ease at all.

WRAP STITCH

A wrap stitch is used to eliminate the hole created when using the short row shaping method. Work to the position on the row indicated in the pattern, wrap the next st (by slipping next st onto right needle, taking yarn to opposite side of work between needles and then slipping same st back onto left needle – on foll rows, K tog the loop and the wrapped st) and turn, cont from pattern.

BEADING

Bead 1 (RS rows) = place a bead by bringing yarn to front (RS) of work and slipping bead up next to st just worked, slip next st purlwise from left needle to right needle and return yarn to back (WS) of work, leaving bead sitting in front of slipped st on RS. Do not place beads on edge sts of rows as this will interfere with seaming and picking up sts.

Beading note

Before starting to knit, thread beads onto yarn. To do this, thread a fine sewing needle (one which will easily pass through the beads) with sewing thread. Knot ends of thread and then pass end of yarn through this loop. Thread a bead onto sewing thread and then gently slide it along and onto knitting yarn. Continue in this way until required numbers of beads are on yarn.

WORKING A LACE PATTERN

When working a lace pattern it is important to remember that if you are unable to work a full repeat i.e. both the increase and corresponding decrease and vice versa, the stitches should be worked in stocking stitch or an alternative stitch suggested in the pattern.

CHART NOTE

Some of our patterns include a chart. Each square on a chart represent a stitch and each line of squares a row of knitting.

When working from a chart, unless otherwise stated, read odd rows (RS) from right to left and even rows (WS) from left to right. The key alongside each chart indicates how each stitch is worked.

FINISHING INSTRUCTIONS

It is the pressing and finishing which will transform your knitted pieces into a garment to be proud of.

Pressing

Darn in ends neatly along the selvage edge. Follow closely any special instructions given on the pattern or ball band and always take great care not to over press your work.

Block out your knitting on a pressing or ironing board, easing into shape, and unless otherwise states, press each piece using a warm iron over a damp cloth.

Tip: Attention should be given to ribs/ edgings; if the garment is close fitting – steam the ribs gently so that the stitches fill out but stay elastic. Alternatively if the garment is to hang straight then steam out to the correct shape.

Tip: Take special care to press the selvages, as this will make sewing up both easier and neater.

CONSTRUCTION

Stitching together

When stitching the pieces together, remember to match areas of pattern very

carefully where they meet. Use a stitch such as back stitch or mattress stitch for all main knitting seams and join all ribs and neckband with mattress stitch, unless otherwise stated.

Take extra care when stitching the edgings and collars around the back neck of a garment. They control the width of the back neck, and if too wide the garment will be ill fitting and drop off the shoulder. Knit back neck edgings only to the length stated in the pattern, even stretching it slightly if for example, you are working in garter or horizontal rib stitch.

Stitch edgings/collars firmly into place using a back stitch seam, easing-in the back neck to fit the collar/edging rather than stretching the collar/edging to fit the back neck.

Straight cast-off sleeves: Place centre of cast-off edge of sleeve to shoulder seams. Sew top of sleeve to body, using markers as guidelines where applicable. Join side and sleeve seams.

Set-in sleeves: Join side and sleeve seams. Place centre of cast off edge of sleeve to shoulder seams. Set in sleeve, easing sleeve head into armhole.

CARE INSTRUCTIONS

Yarns

Follow the care instructions printed on each individual ball band. Where different yarns are used in the same garment, follow the care instructions for the more delicate one.

Buttons

We recommend that buttons are removed if your garment is to be machine washed.

ABBREVIATIONS

K	knit
P	purl
K1b	knit 1 through back loop
st(s)	stitch(es)
inc	increas(e)(ing)
dec	decreas(e)(ing)
st st	stocking stitch (1 row K, 1 row P)
garter st	garter stitch (K every row)
beg	begin(ning)
foll	following
rem	remain(ing)
rev st st	reverse stocking stitch (1 row P, 1 row K)
rep	repeat
alt	alternate
cont	continue
patt	pattern
tog	together
mm	millimetres
cm	centimetres
in(s)	inch(es)
RS	right side
WS	wrong side
sl 1	slip one stitch
psso	pass slipped stitch over
tbl	through back of loop
M1	make one stitch by picking up horizontal loop before next stitch and knitting into back of it
M1p	make one stitch by picking up horizontal loop before next stitch and purling into back of it
yfwd	yarn forward
yon	yarn over needle
yrn	yarn round needle
Mp	Make picot: Cast on 1 st, by inserting the right needle between the first and second stitch on left needle, take yarn round needle, bring loop through and place on left (one stitch cast on), cast off 1 st, by knitting first the loop and then the next stitch, pass the first stitch over the second (one stitch cast off).
Cn	cabl needle
C4B	Cable 4 back: Slip next 2 sts onto a cn and hold at back of work, K2, K2 from cn.
C4F	Cable 4 front: Slip next 2 sts onto a cn and hold at front of work, K2, K2 from cn.

ACKNOWLEDGEMENTS

We would like to convey our warmest wishes of appreciation to our incredible team, Graham Watts for the wonderful photographs and editorial design, Angela Lin for her skills on the page layouts, our three fabulous models, Nichola Radcliffe, Fiona Beck and Hannah Wright, Diana Fisher whose hair and make-up talents ensured they all looked so glamorous, Stella Smith and Sue Whiting, for their pattern writing expertise, Ella Taylor, Sandra Richardson and Arna Ronan for their beautiful knitting, and to Susan Laybourn for her patience in completing the garments so carefully.

Our gratitude also goes to Dorian and Amanda Grayson for allowing us to shoot at their fantastic house and for putting up with the ever changing deadlines, to Lindsay whose support we value so, so highly and last but not least, to Nigel, for the loan of some very essential props.

Thanks to you all for making another book possible, we couldn't have done it without you.

INDEX